BATTLING THE QUITS

BATTLING THE QUITS

E. Todd Stubblefield

CITI OF
BOOKS

CITIOFBOOKS, INC.
3736 Eubank NE Suite A1
Albuquerque, NM 87111-3579
www.citiofbooks.com

Hotline: 1 (877) 389-2759
Fax: 1 (505) 930-7244

Ordering Information:
Quantity sales. Special discounts are available on quantity purchases by corporations, associations, and others. For details, contact the publisher at the address above.

Printed in the United States of America.

| ISBN-13: | Softcover | 978-1-959682-06-6 |
| | eBook | 978-1-959682-07-3 |

Library of Congress Control Number: 2022919298

A SPECIAL THANKS

There are so many friends and family who support me in the various endeavors and ventures of my life that I would like to say thank you to individually, but the numbers are too great; so, with that thank you to all my family and friends for your love and support. Now to my wife Kammie, three children (Alexis, Kamden, and goddaughter Rejoice), granddaughter Jackie, sister Sheila, brother-in-law Lou, Matriarch Aunt Ada, extended sister/cousins Diana and Wanda, mother-in-law Carolyn, father-in-law Frederick, and inner circle (Elder Mike, Elder Stacey, and Jejuan Smith) and my man Deacon Preston and Shelbert who always push me to write my books; thank you all who consistently pushes me to do and be greater - I love you all so much. Thank you for everything you do to help me.

Contents

Introduction

Battling the Quits arises out of the depths of fighting emotionally and spiritually against thoughts and desires of wanting to quit, give up, or throwing in the towel. When we were created in the image of God, a part of our makeup, our chemistry, and psyche was comprised of achieving goals, living dreams, aspiring to new heights, and ultimately living a Christ-centered life. But when Adam fell in the garden of Eden it created a ripple effect that would erode who we are and all of whom we are supposed to be. For this reason, it seems to never fail when trouble and/or adversity rears its ugly head many people's default mechanism is to quit. The Apostle Paul reminds us in Galatians 6:9, "...and let us not grow weary while doing good, for in due season we shall reap if we do not lose heart." What a promise and principle to live by found in the word of God and so timely for such times as these. As children of God, we must be deeply rooted in the word of God and rigidly fixed on His promises. He said, His word shall not return Him void but it shall accomplish that for which it has been sent. His words have been sent to inspire and empower us. This is where our patience must be parked and rested. With that said, it does not matter the magnitude of the storm that is raging in our lives – what matters is the magnitude of the fight that we wage during the storm - do not quit! A season of reaping what we have sown is on its way; strap in, hold on, and never quit – it is not an option.

Hebrews 12:1-2 "...and let us run with endurance the race that is set before us, looking unto Jesus, the author, and finisher of our faith, who for the joy set before Him endured the cross, despising the shame

Chapter 1

WHAT ARE THE QUITS?

It is a somber song, one that has topped the music billboard charts for decades. A song that has been remade and remixed a million plus times as each one of us has sung it. Well, I can personally say I have sung it one too many times myself. The single of course is titled I quit; and there is only one verse accompanied by many excuses – "I quit." Can you count the times the words have glossed your lips? Can you count the times when you were so emotionally overwhelmed by your situation all that came to mind was, I quit. I cannot because it is too numerous and at one point became a default response to some areas of my life. Built-in each of us is that learned behavior of quitting, giving up, walking away, or simply experiencing that gesture of throwing our hands in the air while shaking our heads in frustration. That point in life where this one instance has rattled you so bad that your emotional response was a feeling or desire to cease, discontinue, or stop doing something for one reason or another. What is or what has been your quit(s), do you know? That very thing or combination of things that keeps you awake at night tossing and turning with the mattress becoming your swimming pool of sweat and/or tears. Those things that make you nauseous, weak, frustrated, angry, delirious, nervous, anxious, timid, hesitant, powerless, and the like. It is that thing or combination of things that will push you to your breaking point; to that place of even questioning your walk with your Lord and Savior Jesus Christ. Those times when your heart is beating so hard in your chest that a geologist can measure the seismic vibration as though there is an earthquake within you. What many people do not realize is that quitting is a decision and/or outcome that is emotional and irrational at best. Its temporal relief does not resolve the problem(s) at hand but exasperates it, while the roots of most problems remain intact nourishing the underline or unresolved issue(s). Quitting is also an attitude of weakness and is a thief by nature. It robs us all of one of life's most basic and essential needs to survive and that is stick-to-itiveness - the ability to fight. This false notion of quitting as though it is an answer to life's quarrelsome problems and most tricky situations is equivalent to providing someone a space heater, saying be warm tonight while having to brave the elements of Chicago winters with no other means of cover or shelter; it does not work.

Today, quitting is our common cold, and many people are catching it. It is a disposition of a poisoned spirit killing everything from who we are to whom we desire to become.

Thinking about this, consider the young rich ruler in Matthew 19:16, who asked Jesus a simple question and when the answer was not favorable or to his liking the Bible records, he walked away sad. In other words, he quit his pursuit which was for eternal life because he had no fight for life. Like most people when something is not favorable or to our liking, we give up instead of pursuing or exploring further what was said for clarity or a better understanding. In many instances today we do not put up a fight for what we want or believe in. How many of us miss the marks and/or milestones of life because we lack importunity, perseverance, or the will to push past resistance or the no's in life? Too many opportunities, goals, and dreams are regularly missed today because we have the wrong fight in us. Instead of fighting the good fight of faith and pushing past negative emotions resulting from denial and rejection, people are fighting with attitudes that embrace the quitter's mentality and bear fruit that injures. The more I think about where we are in life today, I encourage you to fight and challenge the no and seek out all answers or possibilities to get to your next level or dreams. Luke chapter 11:9, encourages us all to ask – for it will be given, seek – and we shall find, knock – and the door will be opened. Do not allow hopelessness to douse you with a broken spirit of quitting – battle those thoughts and emotions. Do not walk away from the fight but walk into it fully armored in Christ Jesus knowing that you are a winner, not a quitter.

Now there are times that we will quit, and there will be some for good reasons. One of which comes to mind is when you find yourself fighting someone else's battle; encouraging them not to give up or quit but eventually realizing they are not fighting for themselves. So, you will quit what you are doing to spare yourself the wasted effort. You will get to a point where you want more for a person than they want for themselves. This can be a toxic environment draining you of life. Their frustrations become yours and that is a killer.

Quitting is a weapon that slowly forms against us. Whether it will prosper or not, is all up to us. If we allow seeds of hopelessness which is Christ-lessness to germinate within us, then quitting will prosper. But as King David did, we also must do and that is to encourage ourselves with the word of God then that weapon of quitting becomes dull; pointless, and of no effect. God calls for us to excel beyond the feeling or emotions of quitting. To be victors and not victims. Certainly, there are no expectations of us to be robotic having no feelings or emotions when we are experiencing that notion to quit. But we are expected through Christ Jesus to win and/or be triumphal, over everything that presents itself against us; i.e "...no weapon formed against us shall prosper, and every tongue that rises against us we shall condemn." Without God in our lives, this is impossible. But with God all things are possible, and we win. Through Christ, we defeat the attitude of quitting versus quitting defeating us.

In Christ Jesus, we were never called to be defeated but to be more than conquerors; and this is accomplished through the Holy Spirit who empowers and strengthens us. This does not mean we are without struggle or exempt from troubles; but as children of God, we are wired to press toward the mark of the upward call in Christ Jesus. We are to fight the good fight of faith meaning we are equipped with the full armor of God. However, there are times in our lives when our armor will have chinks in it, and we are worn and withered from the battles of life. We are weakened and that is when our wiring in Christ Jesus as new creations come loose; we find ourselves entertaining those roaming thoughts of the quitter's attitude; this is normal. These are the very thoughts that we are supposed to cast down that exalt themselves against the word and will of God for our lives. 2 Corinthians 10:3-6, says though we walk in the flesh we do not wage war as the flesh does, but we pull down these strongholds immediately. Christ provides us with an excellent example of how to accomplish casting down these strongholds. In Matthew 26; Jesus experienced those feelings that can lead to giving up; but in response to those emotions He said, "...if this cup could pass from Me, not my will but thy will be done." Do not get caught sleeping and weary as Peter, James, and John did. But as Christ prayed, we must also pray to the Lord our strength and withstand the fiery darts of the wicked one. We must believe and trust God that He will make a way of escape in our time of trouble; that in no uncertain terms God has our backs – so we do not have to quit. God tells us in Proverbs 3:4-6 to trust in the Lord with our hearts and lean not to our own understanding, but to acknowledge Him in all our ways and He will direct our paths. So, when your path in life becomes dense because you cannot see the trees from the forest it is because you are leaning on yourself, not trusting in God, and neither are you acknowledging Him in all your ways. God has given you as His child His Holy Spirit who will lead you in all truth and righteousness thus clearing a path of travel for you. Yes, along this cleared path there will be pitfalls, traps, and snares. And yes, we will falter but as the adage would have it, winners never quit, and quitters never win. Which of the two will you be today? A winner or a quitter? It is a mindset, winning and quitting, and the choice is yours. Make the right choice today by choosing to follow Christ and you will never lose and neither will you find yourself fulfilling those desires to quit.

Chapter 2

EXERCISING CHARACTER

Ask yourself this question - how easy is it for you to simply walk away from your dreams, goals, and aspirations when life presents you with a valley or mountain? Do you possess the fortitude, stick-to-itiveness, and/or perseverance to fight for what you believe in? Do you own some stock in that thing called willingness which enables you and me to walk through those valleys and scale those mountains? Does importunity reside within your blood? What many people do not realize is that walking away, quitting, and giving up in many instances are only temporary sedatives to long-term problems. See, our dreams, goals, desires, and aspirations are visions and forecasts of life that make up the whole of who we are and define our character. When these things that drive us manifest, when they show up in our difficulties, they speak volumes about who we are to the world. But if we short ourselves by giving into quitting then our character never develops, and we become the what-ifs of life agonized by unfulfillment; never finding that thing to alleviate the torment that haunts us for not accomplishing something special or great in our lives. That special thing that is accredited to your name. That very thing that defines you. Whether you know it or not, tough times, struggles, pains, restless nights, and difficulties are the exercisers and strengtheners of our character. They are the creamers for our coffee. Those very situations that supply our reservoirs with fortitude and resilience enabling us to draw that extra push from within when striving to reach that said goal, special place, and/or achieving what appeared unachievable. It is so important that we allow our character to be exercised when faced with or experiencing a struggle. Without these exercises, our lives would be wallpapered with quitting and hopelessness which then will become our nesting place.

Breaking through barriers, overcoming obstacles, and scaling unimaginable heights is what makes success and prosperity all worthwhile; and the worthwhile of it all is payment in full when we realize within ourselves that we can achieve the impossible. Let us be honest with ourselves; does it not feel good to know that you did that or that the success of something's being and/or existence is because you played an intricate part in it? Experiencing those emotions and feelings of "I did it" is rejuvenating and there is nothing wrong with that. Yes, there is something wrong with lauding that praise all over yourself not having some humility. Yes, there is something wrong with making others feel less than and being arrogant about your accomplishments is not okay. But to be proud and encouraged because of your achievements is okay. Therefore, simply walking away or quitting when the roads of life become difficult is not optional and neither is a solution. When we make these types of decisions haphazardly to just walk away because of whatever, leaves us empty and filled with nothing; no achievements, no success stories, no accomplishments, no victories to shout about, and no foundation to build upon going forward. For me, I need those shouting moments of victory and sighs of relief when I have gotten past or overcome that struggle. Those moments build within me fortitude and it will for you as well. Those moments when I can yell aloud, thank you Jesus, and praise You God for getting me through those obstacles and over the humps. I know all too well that Quitters are often left with a life of regret and would of, should of, and could of – because I was a card-carrying member of that Quitters Club years ago. Wherein one's mind becomes a garage full of parked dreams, passed-over opportunities, and lifeless possibilities. Unfortunately, many people are unaware that Greatness is a commodity that is afforded to all to experience through God's grace and divine plan. However, God's plan is not automatic, or a given; there are some choices that we all must make about the life we want to live. A life without Christ is one where greatness is left unattended on the tables of despair, hopelessness, and futile living. But a life with Christ is one of limitless possibilities and opportunities that we all should experience and shout about. The Apostle Paul reminds the reader that "*I can do all things through Christ who strengthens me*" (**Phil 4:13**). As for me, I have had my share of days and nights where greatness has escaped me because I quit or gave up on a dream where the road had been less traveled, and the adversity appeared to daunt. Today, I refuse to be marred by a life lacking fulfillment and the joy of accomplishment; therefore, I repeat to myself in those moments when I am challenged beyond my perceived limitations that quitting is not an option – find a way. With that said, thanks be to God that over the years I have come to learn that suffering endures for a night, and joy comes in the morning. That part of scripture that says "suffering endures for a night" speaks to a season of time in our lives; for each of us, those seasons and times are different. But we must experience them in order to build resilience and fortitude in our lives. These are two of the most important attributes and characteristics that we can obtain for the unforeseen journeys that lie ahead. If we do not possess them among other attributes – we become worse than the common cold. Spreading a virus that attacks every aspect of our being; negatively impacting our family, friends, and communities.

Speaking of quitting and its negative impact. I was on vacation in Myrtle Beach, South Carolina when the family and I were checking out this new housing/retail development that had been recommended to us that we should visit. While driving through we decided to stop and walk the area. There was a Barns & Noble bookstore there and I became inquisitive wanting to know if my book which was published in March 2018, (Committed to the Unthinkable), was in stores or was it still an online purchase only. So of course, I walked in with my son and patiently waited near the customer service desk for the next available associate to inquire of my book's status. Ironically, near the customer service booth where I was standing was the Christian section with the Bible's and nationally and internationally known Christian authors. Still waiting to inquire I decided to peruse through the various books on the shelves when out of nowhere the words – battling the quits buried themselves in the inner chambers of my heart. The thought itself could not have come at a better time than it did. God knew what I needed before the need arose. He was storing them up in me as a defense to stave off the thoughts, ideas, and contemplation of giving up and/or walking away from my dreams and goals because of what would soon be a disappointing answer. God knows how easy it is for us to navigate to places of despair and hopelessness when we allow frustrations, weariness, fear and self-destructing patterns, and negative thoughts to set in. As stated earlier, I knew the word quit all too well for there was a season of time wherein quitting had taken up residence in my life and I had lived up to its full expectations and practices. I had become a quitter. Now some people would beg the differ of my assessment of self and ask whenever was I a quitter? And my initial response would be you do not know my inner me. Their assumption would be based on my accomplishments and successes that were evident or better yet that were seen; and what limited things I have allowed others to know and experience about me. What most people do not realize as stated earlier is that quitting is not an action but an attitude; and that the action of quitting is the fruit of that mindset. Quitting is a virus that plagues our souls and had infected my nature and my being. And somehow or another it had embedded itself in my DNA, my x and y chromosomes long after I was born, and was altering my personage. Thank God I was able to divorce myself of it before my children were born. Otherwise, I believe my children would have potentially inherited and/or been raised in a quitting culture; and they would have been defeated in life long before they got started; not because of who they were but because of a toxic environment they would have been raised in or exposed to.

Unbeknown to me, my psyche and outlook on life had been maligned without my permission. Somehow it was as though I had been invaded by a body snatcher; a spirit that was not empowering nor sent from God. I found myself riddled with excuses as to why I was unable to finish what I started; to add insult to injury, I allowed set goals and dreams to be shelved in the recesses of my mind. What is worse is that I would have the desire to do something innovative, creative, or even try something different in life; and before I know it, I found a reason as to why it would not work or an excuse as to why I should not try. Ultimately self-sabotaging my effort, energy, and elasticity to achieve that which I dreamed of. Allow me to say that quitting is a curse from hell destroying the very greatness of whom God created each of us to be in Him. When God laid these words "battling the quits" on my heart they were speaking life to me, empowering, and challenging me to get beyond the expectation of giving up, quitting, or settling for less. The Lord was encouraging me to pray, to talk with Him lest I find myself struggling for answers to keep my dreams and hopes alive. Those very hopes and dreams of one day becoming a household name synonymous with other well-known authors. And let us not forget that part of the dream of being named amongst the Times bestsellers list. Oh, man! Only to see that coming to the past would be life-changing. But that life-changing experience will never become a reality if we do not know how to battle the quits.

As I continued to patiently wait in Barnes & Noble pondering all of this, I had come to the realization that I was in a season of nothing and/or dryness, meaning that things were not moving for me and book sales were far, few, and in between. During such seasons it is easy to get lost and to become despondent although you are an accomplished author. I had to think about it. I had done something that I never imagined I could do. In fact, I did not grow up wanting to be an author or even thought I could author a book. Truthfully speaking, formulating a halfway decent sentence in high school was a challenge. But I did it, I authored a book. That was an awesome season; but like anything else, seasons come and go. And that excitement of being a new author had vanished; and just as quickly as it came it surely went. There was so much more to be accomplished, so much more to be achieved with my book that was lying in state and repose. And the reason there was no movement was simple; I was hoping that God would move the book for me and/or favor me in the evolution of my book. Trust me when I say, God knows where you are and how to elevate you above that place of nothing; when the excitement you once had for something is fleeting faster than you can blink your eyes and the newness has washed away. When no one is celebrating your accomplishments, and your enthusiasm is stolen; God knows how to elevate you. But there are times when it is hard to find that place of joy or excitement again. However, it is during these periods that we must nestle in and settle down for the long haul. God knows our pains and understands our struggles, but He is waiting for you and me to take the next steps by faith and in doing so He will reward and/or favor us with a new season.

Still awaiting the sales associate in Barnes & Noble, I was shortly thereafter asked how can I help you. Without divulging who I was I asked do you all have a copy of "Committed to the Unthinkable" available in the store as cheerful as I could be. He searched their computer and replied – it is a print-on-demand book from the publisher. In other words, you must purchase it, then we order it, then it will be shipped to you. This answer was not anything unexpected, however, a little disappointment crept in as I started thinking about what I must do to get from online to in the stores. I did not want to remain an online order book only, unless the online sales demands are reaching record numbers but at that moment, there was little to nothing happening online for me. With that said, if there are brick-and-mortar bookstores, I need to be on the shelves as well; and at the ready for those who want to purchase a copy and have it immediately in their hands. There was once upon a time I would have walked away from this situation without a second thought while throwing my hands in the air and settled with the answer I received from the sales associate; but not today. Too often I have settled for less in all areas of my life, all in the name of being humble and quote-unquote waiting for something to happen, being patient. Patience is a good thing in the right seasons but there are seasons and times when you will have to get out there and hustle your tail off if you want to see change or experience your dreams. **Proverbs 10:4** says, *"He who has a slack hand becomes poor, but the hand of the diligent makes rich."* I know I am not the only one who has been filling those shoes by settling for less and possessing that slack hand. Truthfully, nothing is going to happen for me if I do not get out there and push the sales and draw interest and attention to my book. It is incumbent for us to get out of this quitting and settling for where things are mindset or better yet living in defeat if we want to be accomplished. Unfortunately, too many of us have this defeatist attitude. We often surrender without a fight, never realizing that the obstacles that are before us are so much inferior to us. Think about it - when we quote scripture, acknowledging that greater is He (Jesus) that is in me than he that is in the world. We are subscribing to the fact that Jesus is not only Lord meaning Master of all things, but that He is also sovereign and controls the universe. If this is a part of our Christian foundation and belief, then we ought to live life in such a manner where quitting is not an option but a redirection when necessary. We must learn to fight and battle the quits; those feelings and emotions of giving up. We must give quitting an uppercut and a right cross to knock it out of our lives or else it will do the same to us.

Sadly, all that I have said thus far will be missed because of blind eyes and deafened ears; causing many to miss the doors of opportunity awaiting all of us to walk through. We are often footsteps away from prosperity, success, abundance, and victory which lies just ahead of us and well within our reach. These doors are yelling and screaming our names wanting us to enter here for what we need and long for. But we cannot see nor hear them because life's struggles and weariness have dulled our senses. Hey y'all, and yes, I know this is not proper grammar but again I say hey y'all, God is awaiting us to live out His word which is a lamp unto our feet and a light unto our path. He will help us navigate through the difficulties, struggles, and processes of what we want to accomplish in life. I am not sure if you are aware, but God finds pleasure in our faith and therefore rewards us with our dreams and goals when we diligently seek Him. He calls into existence the very things that were once a thought or imagination;

He gives them substance and life. God loves and is pleased when we walk in faith. Why? Because faith causes us to solely depend on Him and believe Him in His word. What does scripture say about faith? "It is impossible to please God without faith, for those who come to Him must believe that He is, and is a rewarder of those who diligently seek Him" (**Hebrews 11:6**). So, let us tear down the veil that we have erected in our lives which separates us from God. Veils of defeat, anger, frustration, blame, and discouragement. Time to stoke the flames of our spirit man who ought to burn hot within our hearts and souls stirring up our faith. We must encourage ourselves as coals fed to the boiler of a steam engine locomotive train blasting its whistle and throttled full steam ahead. Hey y'all, and again I say hey y'all, success and prosperity are our future in Christ; but we will never see nor experience them if the flames are flickering at best and there is no word of God within us to kindle the fire. To many of us have become smoldering ashes which soon will become cold like an outdoor grill, not in use; and like that which has filled the graves of so many unknown greats, men, and women whose talents, gifts and abilities are buried as a lost treasure within the cemetery. We cannot afford to miss these blessings stored up for each of us. Therefore, until we plant good seeds things will never change for us. Seeds that produce thoughts that say, I am a multi-millionaire, I am a well-known author, my books are best sellers, I am a great then fill in the blank to whatever your greatness is. Speak to your situation in the affirmative and take actions that align and coincide with those beliefs. We cannot reap where we have not sown, and neither will we sow when we do not believe we can reap. Quitting is not a fruit of God's Spirit, but a fiery dot of the enemy aimed at our hearts and minds.

Galatians 6:7-9 NKJV

[7] Do not be deceived, God is not mocked; for whatever a man sows, that he will also reap. [8] For he who sows to his flesh will of the flesh reap corruption, but he who sows to the Spirit will of the Spirit reap everlasting life. [9] And let us not grow weary while doing good, for in due season we shall reap if we do not lose heart.

So, we have to choose what seeds we will sow. If we choose to sow the seeds of do nothing with our lives, gifts, and talents then we will reap a harvest of nothing. But if we sow seeds of something, then whatever that something is will begin to grow and at the appointed time, we will reap that harvest. So, do not grow weary in well doing nor lose heart, for in due season we shall reap, again I am shouting will reap. In other words, if we do not quit on our goals, dreams, and desires, what we are working for, will come to fruition right before our very eyes. So, let us start reaping by refusing to quit.

Chapter 3

WHEAT AND TARES

The wheat and tare parable in scripture is immensely powerful and thought-provoking as we can see it unfold in everyday life. Wherein these two plants are remarkably similar in nature and appearance and grow together; yet one is poisonous, and the other is good for food. When Jesus uses this analogy to illustrate the similarities between the children of God and those of the world, He warns His harvesters not to be anxious about separating them before the harvest because it is quite easy to mistake one for the other. Furthermore, the tare also attaches itself to the wheat therefore uprooting the tare could uproot and destroy the wheat simultaneously. So, Jesus instructs them, to leave the two together until the appointed time when both will be plucked at harvest and the tare is discarded and the wheat is used. I refer to this parable as a part of battling the quits because as discussed earlier the tares by nature are poisonous plants and their effects can be damaging. No different than the tare, some people can be poisonous in their beliefs and outlook on life which in a similar fashion can be very damaging to others to whom they are attached. So, in battling the quits, wherein we are fighting to ward off and defend against emotions, feelings, and seasons of life where we experience those desires of giving up and quitting, we must consider that some of these experiences are attributed to outside influences that are attached to our lives. I know

Jesus told the harvesters to be patient until harvest time, but as it relates to people, He never said that if you are the wheat and recognize that someone else who is a part of your life is a tare that you could not uproot and/or detach yourself from them. This is important because some people are simply poisonous or have negative attitudes. Their leeching onto and off others can be overwhelming and unsettling for those who are trying to do their best to prosper and succeed in life. Unfortunately, when tares are metaphors for people, these individuals come in many shapes, fashions, and forms. They are family members, significant others, spouses, friends, neighbors, co-workers, and church members. So, we must be incredibly careful when it comes to our circles of influence. With all that said, we might want to look in the mirror to ensure that we are not our own tare or a tare to someone else. Being poisonous with thoughts and beliefs that sabotage our efforts or those of someone else.

Funny, as a Pastor I often see the coziness of the two, the wheat and the tares as they are entwined and are very intimate in the relationship; and please do not mistake intimacy for couples' relationships but the broader scope of those who are close and personal with one another with the wheat never realizing the poison of the tare.

Let us look at this parable in the book of Matthew:

Matthew 13:24-30 NKJV

[24] Another parable He put forth to them, saying: "The kingdom of heaven is like a man who sowed good seed in his field; [25] but while men slept, his enemy came and sowed tares among the wheat and went his way. [26] But when the grain had sprouted and produced a crop, then the tares also appeared. [27] So the servants of the owner came and said to him, 'Sir, did you not sow good seed in your field? How then does it have tares?' [28] He said to them, 'An enemy has done this.' The servants said to him, 'Do you want us then to go and gather them up?' [29] But he said, 'No, lest while you gather

up the tares you also uproot the wheat with them. [30] Let both grow together until the harvest, and at the time of harvest I will say to the reapers, "First gather together the tares and bind them in bundles to burn them but gather the wheat into my barn.""

It is important to note in this parable that when the men had slept that the enemy came in and sowed seeds of tares. How does this happen in the lives of people? Subtleties – when others grow on us with their values and belief even though their values and belief differ from ours. Some intentionally try maligning our beliefs wherein others simply rub off on us. Tares are injurious weeds that look like wheat when it is young but when it matures it can consume and kill other vegetation around them. Now that word slept can be metaphoric for times of being caught off guard, inattentiveness, not being careful, or letting down your defenses. It is during these times that enemies will come into your life and plant bad seeds; and before you know it your lifelong goals, dreams and desires are being sucked out of you. In fact, because of these tares (people), we find ourselves distracted and unconsciously abort or quit on those things that are important to us. Thinking back on a time early in my career as a Deputy Sheriff, one of our high-ranking officials was retiring and she made a comment about me. She took a shot at me in that she said that I never accomplish or finish what I start. Those words hurt my heart, in fact, they cut me deep. Shots were fired and the target was hit successfully. I was crushed. I wanted to take aim back at her and fire harmful and assaultive words, but what good or purpose would that serve? So, I did not. However, I did consider her words for years while weighing myself to see if any of this was true and, in some areas, she was correct, spot on. And instead of doing something about what was true in some areas of my life, I slept on I and ignored them. And while I slept, those seeds germinated and took root in my life. I look back now, some twenty to thirty years later, I see hundreds of things that I left unaccomplished and that is tragic.

Unfortunately, and regrettably, at one period in my life, I was the tare in my life. I was sowing a variety of seeds that were to my disadvantage leading to harvests of nothing. I not only failed to recognize what I was doing but I also made excuses and complained as to why all these terrible things were happening to me.

As quoted earlier and I quote again.

Galatians 6:7-9 NKJV

[7] Do not be deceived, God is not mocked; for whatever a man sows, that he will also reap. [8] For he who sows to his flesh will of the flesh reap corruption, but he who sows to the Spirit will of the Spirit reap everlasting life. [9] And let us not grow weary while doing good, for in due season we shall reap if we do not lose heart. …

This scripture and principle of sowing and reaping applies to every facet of our lives and is often overlooked or missed when it manifests itself; even to the extent that when a bad harvest comes most people never realize that what they are experiencing is from a seed that they had sewn some time earlier in life.

One thing I have come to learn is that victory, success, and the ability to overcome are all mine to lose. I have them in Christ Jesus, but it is up to me to keep them, walk in them, and live them out in every phase of life. We have a choice as to what life we want to live; one of wheat or tares. We have a choice as to what seeds we want to plant, those that produce a harvest that is good or those that are bad; but at the end of the day, it is a choice. So, battle the quits and plant seeds that are good and life-giving.

Chapter 4

IT NEVER FAILS

Sure enough, it never fails that someone always quits or falls by the wayside of life over things that are simple in nature. What are your options and why is quitting one of the answers to the multiple-choice question in your life? Possessing that fighter's mentality and mindset of battling the quits when adversities and/or challenges arise is essential to everyday life. Why did I quit? I will explain momentarily as we build into this chapter. My AAU Team and I were at the BigShots Basketball tournament in Myrtle Beach, South Carolina, and yep it happened, one of my players fell by the wayside, or for all intent and practical purposes he walked out on the team at the end of a game. Mind you it is the second to the last tournament of the season so leaving at this point has no real consequences, cost, or bearings on him; at least that is what he thought. But the truth be told he had already given up before he walked out on us at the tournament. In many instances, the desire to quit happens long before the action does. Our minds have often visited this place in our lives and are made up about the decisions we are going to make long before we make them. Case and point! Something is not working in your favor, or we do not like the direction in which things are heading for us; so, various thoughts and plans of action begin to formulate about what we are going to do next if things do not change for the better or if they continue heading south. Now, there are some instances where we do not have a choice and must make these decisions of quitting or walking away for the good of all. However, in many others, these are our defeated moments and we have already set in motion the decision to quit. Unfortunately for my player, somewhere unbeknown to him he had already quit before the season had begun. Even better it could be just the opposite in that no one has taught him how to fight through the adversities of life or how to battle those emotions and/or feeling of quitting. With that said, as stated earlier we were in Myrtle Beach, South Carolina at the BigShots basketball tournament. We were in the semi-finals and all we had to do was win that game and we would be playing for the championship the next day, but our boys were being whipped physically and mentally. So, I subbed this young man in for another player who was struggling. This was his opportunity to shine and change the momentum of the game. One principle or train of thought I have always shared with my players is that it does not matter who starts the game or how much playing time you receive. What matters is that you maximize the opportunity and finish strong. Well, he did not do that. In fact, he did not do anything different to positively impact the game. He did just the opposite- he added to the demise of the game by having three consecutive turnovers, coupled with getting beat up and down the court. His body language began to speak loudly I quit. So, I pulled him out of the game just as fast as I put him in. Yes, he was mad and like always nothing is ever his fault. This is the type of player you cannot coach or in other terms, they are not coachable. These types of players are riddled with excuses as to why he or she is not performing well; and how everyone else is wrong except them. To add to his emotional escapade, he felt he was not getting enough playing time which was nothing more than the fuel he needed to add to the forest fire that was already burning out of control in his life. Too often young and/or immature athletes measure or equate their success with either the amount of playing time they are receiving or if they are starting the game or not. True success can be measured in so many ways. But for athletes, it should never be measured by one's playing time or by who does or does not start the game. It should be measured by one's contribution to the team's mission and goals. My football scholarship was not because of me being a starter because I did not a starter. However, when I got into the game, I played hard and played well. I took full advantage of every moment I stepped on that field and made the coaches think twice before pulling me out of the game. And when they pulled me out, they made sure I stood right beside them to go right back into the game. So, I maximized my opportunity and finished strong each time.

So yes, my player quit on us but why did I quit on my player? Quitting can be a two-way street. I should have not only known better, but I should have also done better. I should have fought for him and not against him. This is part of the problem in our culture wherein it is easier to fight a battle against one another when we should be fighting for each other. What did I expect? To know better when even I had not done better. Though he was 18 years old, an adult by society's standards, he was still a kid trying to figure out life and I failed him in my part of his life. This young man lost his father several years before and I did not know of any older brothers that were there or not to help him adjust to his loss and navigate the pitfalls of life. As I think back, I should have fought for him. He is the younger and I am the older. I understand life a little better than he does greater than he and should not have let him go as easily as so many of us have done to one another. My Lord, I quit and at that time I did not realize that quitting was still a part of my life, but it was. I know his behavior was not fully my responsibility, but coaching is more than the x's and o's, wins and losses, likes and dislikes. It is about empowering, mentoring, and shaping the lives of those who are in your care for those brief moments in life; and frankly speaking, I failed to do that for him.

Turning back to the beginning of the season, this young man was a starter not because he was the better player but because he was my returning point guard from the previous year and I was given an opportunity to show leadership and grow from his previous seasons but that did not happen. Unfortunately, I had to remove him from the starting line after the first two tournaments of the season because he received a technical foul in each tournament; then he was ejected from one of the games for receiving two technical fouls in that game. This was a character issue that had been developing in him for some time now. I was hoping things would be better for him that season than the season before. But the same issues started manifesting early so I dealt with them early. Your hope as a coach is that in the instance of having to discipline your player, he or she would grow from the experience and use it as an opportunity to fight hard to get back to a positive light. But in today's time, people would much rather quit and settle for nothing than fight for something better. And true enough, from the time I removed him from the starting line up everything about him began to diminish. To his credit, he tried to do a little better, but he would always find a way to do something wrong that would bring unnecessary attention to himself, and at some point, he was destined to quit. However, in these moments and times in life, we must learn to go the extra mile with people.

With that said, I do not want to make this chapter all about my basketball player's issues when we all have them. He is no different from many of us when we are faced with difficulties, challenges, and adversities. Quitting at some point becomes a part of the equation. Do not get me wrong, sometimes quitting is a necessity when it comes to having peace of mind. Sometimes it is a necessity when it comes to creating space and/or a means of gathering yourself. But it should never enter the equation of our decision-making process at the beginning or is the end all or be all. If so banish or shelve that thought quickly. Do not entertain it because the more you think about it, the easier it becomes to do so. Too many of us at the first sight or sign of trouble are ready to bail out, jump ship or pack up our toys in the sandbox and roll out. As stated earlier in this book, I know this firsthand because I have done it too often only to later realize I have missed my breakthroughs, my blessings, and my opportunities to grow and my abilities to develop and mature. That growth that we miss is the growth that leads to stamina, perseverance, and importunity; these are the attributes obtained when we learn to stand and fight. It is important that we learn early on to overcome those emotions and feelings of defeat. If we do not learn these things when we are young it becomes that much more difficult to do when we become older. We need that growth that fortifies us against future struggles, trials, and tribulations. Too often victory and success lie at our door awaiting our answer as they knock but we miss their visitation because we allow our pains and struggles to cloud our vision, judgments, and decisions. I love it when the Apostle Paul says in 1 Corinthians 15:57-58, "Thanks be to God Who gives us the victory through Jesus Christ,…". In other words, God positions His children in Jesus Christ to have success or a superior position to rise above adversity, opposition, or difficulty; however, we must be steadfast, immovable, and always abounding in the works of the Lord. So, the thing we must consider and understand is that God does not excuse us from the confrontation but tells us to stand because we have the victory.

In reviewing Matthew 19 again, when Jesus encounters the young rich ruler who begs the question of Jesus of what must he do to inherit eternal life? Jesus takes him through this litany of questions about keeping the commandments and the young rich ruler says to Him all these I have kept from my youth and ask what else was he still lacking. Jesus responds, go sell all you have and give to the poor and come follow me. The Bible records that this young man was left with great sorrow because he had great riches. Often our narrow vision about situations in our lives limits our ability to see the bigger picture or experience a greater opportunity. This view of selling all that he had was dismal. His possession made him who he was, and selling all appeared insurmountable. See Jesus, answered his question to expand his horizons and abilities to be greater and not to be diminished. The young rich ruler's life was defined by the right now and he could not see beyond that. That is how so many of us live our lives today, especially in the African American community. Because we have been disenfranchised, marginalized, robbed of opportunities, systemically oppressed, and everything else leaving many of us to live for the right now not considering that we often shortchange our future. What the young rich ruler did not recognize in that moment of Jesus' answer was that Jesus did not strip him of his abilities, gifts, and/or talents to be rich. Jesus simply wanted to strip him of a false sense of superficial living. If he would have sold all that he had as Jesus answered him, he would not have been poor; but would have become rich in Christ and still maintained his financial wealth. Riches are an internal possession not external. **Proverbs 23:7**, "***For as he thinks in his heart, so is he…***" - so, your thoughts are keenly connected to either your derailment or fulfillment in life. Jesus wanted to take him to a new level of riches that were born out of Kingdom principles that rises far above worldly ones, such as what He wants for all of us. This young man is not alone in his position because what is being required of him is truly a tall order when you have a narrow view of life. My basketball player's vision was narrow, and he could not see above the limited playing time he received; he quit and walked away. All of who he was, was encapsulated at that moment. If only he could have risen above that instance and used it to possess a bigger picture, he would have gained a greater advantage in life. But again, I quit on him as well and failed to help him acquire that bigger picture in life. So, we both quit, and boy do I regret that moment in life, My Lord! I could have helped him jump-start his life in such a manner that he could accomplish whatever he set his mind to despite life's storms. What an invaluable lesson for us all to learn; that quitting is a character killer, a blessing blocker, and in some instances a two-way street.

Where is this young man today? I have no idea but if I see him, I will apologize for not fighting for him and inquire as to how he is doing. As for me, I am seeing better and thinking better about my life personally and the role I play in the lives of others. Where are you? Are you victorious or experiencing a life riddled with quitting? Remember when I said the Apostle Paul said we must be steadfast; well, that means unwavering, rigidly fixed in direction. So, we cannot afford to allow our adversities to cause us to be in doubt. He said, we must be immovable; that means not swayed by our feelings or emotions. Therefore, we must look beyond those errant feelings, emotions, or even what others think about us and put our trust in God, knowing that God rewarded those who diligently seek Him. Then Paul says, we must always be abounding in the works of the Lord. This means to be full and overflowing in effectiveness, influence, and power to make things happen. Without these three attributes we will be consumed by life; and unfortunately, this is where so many people fail and fall short today. We do not have to live in this condition of defeat or with a quitting attitude. In Christ we are winners but in self-righteousness, we will lose.

Chapter 5

STICKS AND STONES MAY BREAK MY BONES, BUT WORDS WILL NEVER HURT ME!

Whoever said that words do not hurt is not only lying to you but also to themselves. Words matter, make no mistake about it. They have the power to build and sustain us psychologically and/or tear us down emotionally. Thinking back to the days of my youth, I can remember that ole childhood saying, "sticks and stones may break my bones, but words will never hurt me" as we attempted to console ourselves after someone obliterated our feelings. Where did such a fable begin, and where does its origin lie? A child's tale indeed is where such a saying finds its beginnings. We all know that words are impactful, powerful, empowering, and life-changing. In a day, they can motivate you to climb the highest of mountains and in the very same instance mow you down like a blade of grass. Words give life and they also take it. Surgically, they can cut away the mass that is cancerous to your spirit, soul, and emotions and equally cut you to the loss of your soul. Having been on the receiving end of such tirades as well as the giver has taught me all too well to be careful, cautious, and wise in what I say and how I say it. I can still feel some of the residual effects from the hurt and the damage they caused me over the years and see what I have caused over the years to others. In fact, we all have seen the effects words have on people when they are the hunted, the prey in the crosshairs of the Fowler's bow, and/or the focus of someone else's verbal assault. Yes, words can be painful, and their sting has taken down the mightiest of people, like sunken warships whose hulls have been compromised by the enemy's torpedoes. Those very fiery darts of words whose intent is meant to steal, kill, and destroy people's lives.

To answer my earlier question as to where that ole saying "sticks and stones may break my bones, but words will never hurt me" finds its origin. Its earliest recording was in 1862. It was from the Christian perspective of taking the high road when someone has been verbally assaulted. Following 1862, the phrase worked itself into schoolyards and/or playgrounds as a response to verbal bullying. Today it has etched its place in American history, but its intention of taking the high road has slowly eroded and faded over the years into the distant past. In fact, it is no longer a road to take. Talk about having to battle the quits, let someone say something to you that strikes a painful chord, and watch the thoughts that creep into your mind. Thoughts that choke out goodness, moral high roads, and everything that is pure in you. Why? Because words hurt. Words can make you quit on everything that you worked hard to be and/or achieve. They can make you want to throw your hands up and walk out on your beliefs and all civility, and run the paths of the flesh. They can be dream killers and vanquish all hope of something better. But no different than words can destroy they can also be the balm that heals and mends those places that were or are broken. They can charge and electrify you at that moment when all else seems to fail. They can be lyrics to a war cry, a chant of invincibility, or those soft whispers that navigate the long nights. This is what I love about the Word of God and its effect on our lives. The Word of God causes us to champion the battle and overcome the desire to quit. Jeremiah the young prophet likens God's Word to a burning fire in his heart that is shut up in his bones (Jeremiah 20:9). God's word caused Jeremiah to rise above his feelings of giving up and walking away from the assignment God sent him on.

Today, we increasingly hear of instances where people are striking back with violent tendencies as so many have exited the high roads of life because of painful words. Again, the power of words is found in Proverbs 18:21, "*The power of life and death are in the tongue*". As stated earlier, words can kill as well as give life. I will never forget the court case a few years back where a high schooler was on trial for verbal bullying. Her words pierced deep into the heart of a young man whom she was involved with in some type of relationship. Her words killed him emotionally destroying the fabric of his being and causing him to quit on life. She had texted him some absurd number of times to just kill herself and he did just that. What a tragedy! Her words had that much impact on that young man's life. With that much power and influence can you imagine what life may have been like for him if that young lady would have used her words to encourage and inspire him? I believe the skies would have been the limit for him simply because he believed in her words.

There was a season of time when many of us were very resilient-and taking the high roads was commonplace - uttering that phrase sticks and stones may break my bones but words will never hurt me" but not today. Verbal bullying has replaced Cupid's arrow of love striking the heart with much poison and pain. That arrow that once represented love has become venomous, laced with hate and destructive intent. Too many lives are lost because people are quitting, giving up, or simply checking out. Words hurt and again I say words hurt no matter who you are. And sometimes when those verbal badgering, attacks, or thoughtless expressions flood our lives we shut down and quit. But I want to encourage you to fight and continue to fight every day regardless of what and/or whom you face; God is bigger.

The Bible reminds us in Proverbs 15:1, that a soft or gentle answer turns away strife, but a harsh answer stirs up anger. Believe me when I say I have been on both sides of these aisles wherein I was the recipient of some harsh answers and other times I have fired them off to others. Neither of the instances was good because they led to some frustration and attacks wherein someone is always emotionally damaged. It does not require much of any of us to be a little more patient, gentler, and kinder in how we approach one another. These venomous attacks on employees, loved ones, friends, associates, and the person whose path we cross is fruitless and honestly despicable. When it comes to a person with authority over another who feels they can fire off at will regardless of the damages; they are foolish. Honestly, it is poor judgment and lacks appreciation for those who are under their care and tutelage. So, we all should be mindful of how we treat one another and choose the road of esteeming others more highly than ourselves. Philippians 2:3-4, says "Let nothing be done through selfish ambition or conceit, but in lowliness of mind let each esteem others better than himself. (4) Let each of you look out not only for his own interest but also for the interest of others. Remember once our lips open and the words begin to fly, we cannot retract our statements, and when they find their mark the damage is done and sometimes irreparable. With that said, feel free to fire off at me words that are loving, peaceful, encouraging, and the sort; but all others you can keep to yourself, and I will do likewise.

Considering this, words create visual images in the minds of the recipient. If what you are saying is negative, then the impact can be very damaging because they not only hear what you are saying but they can also imagine it. The same holds true for words that are positive; the impact can be empowering. Therefore, let us all consider and choose our words wisely, thus minimizing negative effects and maximizing powerful impacts.

Chapter 6

CHOOSING TO DO NOTHING

I was home one evening thinking about the bible study I have been blessed to teach Monday thru Friday in the mornings on Facebook live; and during that thought, the Lord brought to my attention that there is a behavior and attitude of choosing to do nothing. That, in essence, people, are choosing to live in nothing. That is people are choosing to be of no importance, significance, or magnitude; that which amounts to nothing. Christ did not die for us to live out such a life deemed as nothing. If no one else recognizes you, you must recognize within yourself that you are relevant and important. That is a hidden treasure that is meant to bless the world. After God dropped this thought into my heart, I immediately began to seek Him out on this when He led me to John 14. Yes, there are seasons when we are to be still and do nothing. But there is a problem when this becomes an attitude. Because our attitudes lead to behaviors, and behaviors become actions, and actions reflect our character, and our character is that by which we are defined and measured in life.

In the book of John, chapter 14, Jesus begins to announce His departure and He encourages the disciples with this verse "...*let not your heart be troubled, if you believe in God also believe in Me for in My Father's house there are many mansions; If it were not so, I would have told you. I go to prepare a place for you. And if I go and prepare a place for you, I will come again and receive you to Myself; that where I am, there you may be also.*" As I pondered this thought that He left with the disciples I began to realize that His leaving was necessary and purposeful. John 16:7, Jesus *"Nevertheless I tell you the truth. It is to your advantage that I go away; for if I do not go away the Helper will not come to you; but if I depart, I will send Him to you."* Jesus tells us it is to our advantage that He leaves. Often contemplating this thought "It is to our advantage that He goes away" - Why? Why is it to my advantage that our Lord and Savior goes away? What do I gain from Him leaving us on earth where there is chaos, pain, and suffering; this place that is overrun with evil and wickedness? Initially, it did not make sense to me. But now, I see and understand better why He needed to go. The Holy Spirit, Who, is God working in us (Ephesians 3:20); would only come after the completed work of Christ on the earth. He, the Holy Spirit, would be the means by which the completed work of Christ is sustained in us, He keeps us until the appointed time of Christ's return. However, this is not a time of idleness. While we yet live and await Christ's return, our lives are supposed to evolve, thrive, shine, and reflect Him through the Holy Spirit. That we would mature and become that new creation in Christ Jesus empowered by the Holy Spirit to do a great work; which is contrary to a life of nothing. This greatness that I speak of is not measured by the accomplishment of others but by the impact, you leave on the lives of all who come into your company. Because of the Holy Spirit's dwelling with and in us, there should be a dynamic stirring up of our lives spiritually. This appointed time was not intended to be a period of idleness or inactivity, but a time in which Jesus was to be seen in our lives. That our character should scream loudly that Jesus is Lord.

So, Jesus tells the disciples in John 14, "*most assuredly, I say to you, he who believes in Me the work that I do he will do also; and greater works than these he will do, because I go to My Father. And whatever you ask in My name that I will do that the Father may be glorified in the Son.*" This is not a time to choose to do nothing when Jesus has given us the how and ability to do wonderful, great, and mighty things. Wherein we have been given the Holy Spirit Who will lead us in this process. It pains me when I see so many people who have settled and given in to nothingness. Christ has positioned us in Him to succeed and prosper. He tells the disciples that He would not leave them as orphans but would pray to the Father and He will give them another Helper, that He would abide in them and with them forever. The very Holy Spirit who now resides in us. Jesus did not come to live life for us but to give us life to be lived in Him. In John 10:10, Jesus deemed this life in Him as the more abundant life.

Interestingly, if someone sends another to help you, to walk you through the process, then they are genuinely interested in your success, growth, development, advancement, and achievement. The first Helper was Christ Who paid the cost of our debt of sin and reconciled us to God through the cross. The second Helper Who is the Holy Spirit; is purposed to seal us in that reconciliation, coupled with being with us forever. He will comfort, advocate, and teach us all things in Christ. He will also lead us in all truth and righteousness. Therefore, wherein the first Helper Christ gives us life, the second Helper will empower us in abundant life. But if we choose to do nothing then we become fruitless missing out on the abundance of Christ Who is our Life.

So, what is that abundant life in 12-17, when He says, ***most assuredly, I say to you, he who believes in Me, the works that I do he will do also, and greater works than these he will do, because I go to My Father. And whatever you ask in My name, that I will do, that the Father may be glorified in the Son.*** What is Jesus saying here? Beginning with most assuredly speaks in turns of an insurance policy that is enforced upon various conditions arising. He gives us the authority to use His name in His absence and fills us with His Spirit so that we may live out that Christ-like experience. Here is where things get interesting, Jesus said the works in which He did we will also do and even greater works than these. So, how can we choose to live in nothing? How dare we allow ourselves to be relegated to insignificance, worthlessness, and of no importance?

The word **works:** to act or operate effectively, to have an effect or influence, to achieve or win by work or effort – the power to produce results.

See when Jesus gave us the Holy Spirit, He gave us the power of God to achieve or win by work or effort. He gave us the power to produce results. This power is enforced when we do, whatever we are doing in the name of Jesus (Col 3:17 & 23). If you look at Ephesians 3:20; God's power (the Holy Spirit) works on the inside of us – to bring about changed conditions in our lives. So, there is an expectation of us during this period of Jesus's physical absence to do great works. This mindset of choosing to do nothing is outside the will of God. In Matthews 25:14-30, Jesus likens the Kingdom of God to a man traveling to a far country, who called His servants and delivered His goods to them. This is speaking exactly to John 14, when Jesus says I go away to prepare a place for you. Oh my gosh, the man who goes to the far country has an expectation of his servants to be wise, to win, and to achieve by work. In fact, two of the three servants took what was given to them and produced more of it wherein one chose to do nothing. When the man returned from his journey, he found that two servants produced in his absence, and he rewarded them with more. But the one who chose to do nothing, was stripped of what he had and kicked him out of his presence into suffering. When Jesus went on His journey to a far country, His Father's house, He delivers to us a gift, the Holy Spirit (Luke 11:9), and the authority to use His name so that we might win and achieve whatever we set out to do. How then is it that the body of Christ is struggling? He asked this question in Luke 18:8; when He returns will He really find faith in the earth?". Why did Jesus ask this question? What does He see that you and I do not? Ask yourself if Jesus returned today what would He find you doing? Would you be living by the power of the Holy Spirit? Would you be battling the quits or giving up or into your struggle or difficulty? Do not choose to live this life without influence or impact, you were created wonderfully and fearfully to be great in Christ Jesus. So now what? Immerse yourself in the word of God and experience the move of the Holy Spirit. Ask God for His revelation pertaining to your life; and how to implement His will in your life. In doing so the Holy Spirit, Who is the very power of God will rest, rule, and abides in you and great things will begin to flourish in you.

Chapter 7

DON'T YOU DO IT!

Don't you do it is a chapter that addresses the appeals or urges to quit something that you have dreamed, desired, and wished for. When hopelessness and thoughts of despair have flooded your being causing the road ahead to appear to be blocked and/or too difficult to travel is not necessarily a sign to quit. There are times when quitting becomes a necessary tool to redirect one's efforts. But quitting should never be the first option in our troubled situations. And if it is your default choice, this is indicative of being too familiar with the practice of quitting and being satisfied with its results. Unfortunately, this is the case for many today and it is becoming more and more commonplace for society. It is not uncommon to hear these words uttered "I don't have to accept, stand for, or take this from you; I quit" or something of the sort. This is where we are today when people simply pack up and roll out; grabbing their toys from the sandbox and jet. Where are those men and women who know how to persevere? Somewhere, the will to fight for what one loves, believes in, or hope for has escaped them. And it appears that no sooner than one person does it, it empowers so many others to follow suit. It is almost like hypnosis, and no one has a mind of their own or dares to be different. Battling the quits means we must muster up the strength to fight off those urges and desires to do the easy thing of giving up and walking away. Again, I sometimes understand the need to quit when we are reassessing some failed areas of our lives. But to become quitters by nature is unacceptable and yes, it's hard to fight when your countenance has fallen but God has positioned us to be fighters, warriors, and mighty people. Philippians 4:13, reminds us that we can do all things through Christ Jesus who strengthens us, so fight. These are not mere words written in the Bible to tickle our fancy but are words that gives life to the hearer. Romans 10:17 says "faith comes by hearing and hearing by the words of God." So, I understand when the non-Believer throws in the towel, waves the white flag, or raises their hands in the air signaling surrender; but for the children of God where is our good fight of faith? Instead of quitting, speak life to your situations. The Bible tells us that life and death are in the power of the tongue – choose your words wisely. This is most important when no one is rooting you on, tooting your horn, or drum majoring your cause we must fight. Encouragement, Motivation, and Inspiration must be the foundation, framework, and furnishings of our lives. Stop making the first straw you draw the quit straw and battle this thing. At no point in our lives can we afford to develop the customs and practices of such principles as quitting, giving up, and having no hope of seeing brighter days. Developing attitudes of defeat will never lead us to the winner's circles of life nor will such behaviors ever be pleasing to God or satisfying to you.

I love it when the words don't you do it are uttered to toddlers who are challenging your authority. Toddlers do not know they are challenging you, but their present course of action is unknowingly dangerous, and the parents have to protect them from themselves – "don't you do it or no!". Can't you see it or have you ever experienced when a toddler is bucking your command? In some sense, it is kind of funny and cute, but it is also the time to establish your authority over the situation and implement best practices in that child's life. The unsettling look, the stern commands coupled with some type of immediate disciplinary actions like popping their little hands will eventually imprint upon the child that something is not right. If you have never seen or experienced this before it is funny and cute and at the same time heartbreaking because good parents never enjoy disciplining their children but understand that there are times when it is warranted. Here is an example of how it sometimes unfolds. Your child who is either crawling or barely walking is inching towards something that could be dangerous, painful, or may cause some discomfort. As you notice it you begin to say no to draw their attention away from the hot stove, the staircase, or from touching something that potentially is hazardous or may create a mess. For a moment they stop and look at you smiling. Then suddenly they are back on their way, and you say aloud with a little more emphasis on your voice no or don't you do it or do that. As cited earlier you break their attention for a moment and just as quickly as before they are on their mission to do what you told them not to do because they simply do not understand you or the conditions of the present situation. Now you have found that you have to swiftly take action such as repeating your commands sternly coupled with a quick popping of their little hand and/or removing them from harm's way. Their crying and their tears break your heart, but it was a necessary action because the child does not understand the danger and consequences of their actions.

This parallels with the thoughts of quitting or giving up wherein you are faced with something that appears to be insurmountable or unattainable and now you find yourself on the avenue of defeat; entertaining the thoughts of quitting or giving up. The Holy Spirit is yelling don't you do it, because the consequences are far greater than you can imagine. As the thoughts are entertained, mulled over, and contemplated your next decision will have a major bearing on your future. Trust me when I say, Adam and Eve could have never imagined the consequences of their action when they disobeyed God. Adam was given a set of instructions by God, whom I believe Adam gave to his wife Eve. She knew right from wrong but like a child could never have imagined that her actions would impact humanity as they have. In Eve's discussion with the serpent, she told him that God said, we shall not eat it nor shall you touch it, lest you die. I could only wish that God would have raised His voice loudly, saying don't you do it, no! Then popped her hands, as they stretched out to grab that fruit. But in doing so, His direct involvement would have eliminated free will which is contrary to God's love. If we only read God's word daily, we would defeat that which is set out to defeat us. Therefore, chase your dreams! Pursue your goals! Accomplish your heart's desires! These are life rewards given by God when we live by faith. So don't you do it! Do not take the easy road as so many do. Fight and enjoy victory when your breakthrough comes.

Chapter 8

WHAT ARE YOU DOING HERE ELIJAH?

1 Kings 19:9, *"And there he went into a cave, and spent a night in that place; and behold the word of the Lord came to him, and He said to him, what are you doing here Elijah?"*

I love this scripture as it unfolds because Elijah somewhat epitomizes our lives in the sense that one minute, we are praising God, high on life, and moments later we find ourselves running for our lives. Elijah was on the run for forty-one days attempting to put as much distance between him and Jezebel who had just threatened his life. He had just stood as the mouthpiece of God condemning King Ahab and Israel, and witnessing God put to death the false prophets of Baal whom Jezebel had installed over Israel. Elijah was God's man sent to deliver His people from idolatry, wickedness, and the evil that Jezebel brought upon the people and the land. She was a treacherous woman and in some sense one to be feared and to be weary of. She was merciless, ruthless, and vile; simply pure evil. I am sure we all are familiar with someone of like manner who causes your skin to crawl. Who, like Elijah, has had us on the run fearing threats and painful possibilities. Funny enough, she is probably the reason why we have marathon runners today; and Elijah was the first of them. 1 Kings19:1-3, records it all wherein King Ahab, tells Jezebel that Elijah had put to death all 450 prophets of Baal, and Jezebel was livid and sent a messenger to Elijah saying in verse 2; "So let the gods do to me, and more also, if I do not make your life as the life of one of them by tomorrow about this time." She was nasty and feared by all. Verse 3 said, "And when he saw that, he arose and ran for his life...". When he saw what? Elijah envisioned and internalized the message seeing his life as one of the false prophets who had just been killed by God. Therefore, the marathon began. Elijah ran for a day, and then an additional forty days after eating the food provided to him by the angel of the Lord. Allow me to pause right here! You talk about sustaining power! If you look at 1 Kings19:5-8 you will see where the angel of the Lord made provisions for Elijah and instructed him to eat for the journey was too great for him. So, whatever was in that cake baked on coal and water had not only sustaining power but horsepower too. Verse 8 says Elijah went in the strength of the food forty days and forty nights. Again, let the marathon begin and he was on the run until he arrived at Horeb the mountain of God, and entered a cave; then the Lord asked him, what are you doing here? God already knows the answer so why ask the question? Because there is no justifiable reason why Elijah had been running for forty-one days and is now hiding. God was his shield and buckler, Elijah's exceedingly great reward; therefore, he should have pushed back against her idle threats and seen her life become one of those 450 prophets, not his. If for no other reason than God is the same yesterday, today, and forevermore Elijah should have withstood her as he withstood the 450 prophets; and for these same reasons, we must learn how to stand as well – and stop running and quitting at the sign of trouble. We all know that life is not easy and never will be – but these hiccups and valleys cannot be our reason to quit, give up, and/or give in factors – God is our protector, provider, and peace.

As stated, God asked him what are you doing here? Elijah replies, in essence, he was alone, that no other prophets remained. It was as though he was in a pity party and quite often these are the very same conditions, we find ourselves in when trouble arises. At some point in our lives, we must rid ourselves of excuses and simply be honest as to why we find ourselves in self-inflicted conditions. Now, everything is not our fault, we do encounter challenges and circumstances that are external, but we must know the differences between what we are and what we are not solely responsible for, and stop making excuses for our situations. This fear that we have, God did not give to us. 2 Timothy 2:7 says, "For God has not given us a spirit of fear, but of power and of love and of a sound mind." Did you notice the word spirit was not capitalized but lowercase which is indicative of the fact that He is not speaking of the Holy Spirit; but points to your make up as a person created by Him? If God had given you and I a spirit of fear, then it would have nullified His word in Genesis 1:26-28. "Let us make man in Our image and according to Our likeness; let them have dominion over...". The word spirit here speaks to an attitude or principle that inspires, animates, or pervades thought, feeling, or action. In another definition the word spirit is the soul or heart as the seat of feelings or sentiments, or as prompting action. Elijah, what are you doing here?

Who and/or what has you on the run, hiding out? This spirit did not come from God! One of our greatest enemies is the one who lives with us. There are times we will find ourselves on the run from what is required of us in responsibility, relationships, and reality. We hide and run from what it takes. I do not know about you but when I perceive or imagine myself in some unsettling situation, I get a little anxious, antsy, and nervous. All kinds of thoughts begin to race through my mind. I find myself unsettled in my ways and find that I am all over the place. And of course, with those loose thoughts come bad decisions. In times past I have even gone into hiding, hiding in plain sight. Where I am pretending that all is good but internally, I am suffering and struggling to put on a good front. Well, often the action of hiding is an expression of fear, inferiority, low esteem, lacking confidence, powerlessness, weakness, shame, and at the end of the day lacking control of one's own ability to confront what's ahead. So, we put on airs or fronts as though all is well when all hell has broken loose in our lives, and we do not know what to do or how to handle our hellish conditions. So, we run from what is before us and hide in plain sight. Others look upon our smiles as we mask our pain, suffering, and torment. Wanting help all the while but in fear of what others will think. What are you doing here Elijah? This is the question I have asked myself in times past as I have battled with some of life's woes, troubling times, and conditions of hiding in plain sight. Interestingly one of the most common places to hide in plain sight is in church. In fact, Proverbs 5:12-14, "...I was on the verge of total ruin, In the midst of the assembly and congregation". Although this scripture pertains to another issue of life, can you imagine how many other people there are who attend church on the regular sitting next to you Sunday in and Sunday out whose lives are on the verge of total ruin? I have personally seen those days of hiding in church as my mind was invaded by all kinds of crazy thoughts as I hid in the praise and worship. I was on the verge of total ruin in the midst of the assembly and congregation. To think, how many others are in like conditions Sunday in and Sunday out? God's word tells us in Joshua 1:8-9, "This Book of the Law shall not depart from your mouth, but you shall meditate in it day and night, that you may observe to do according to all that is written in it. For then you will make your way prosperous and then you will have good success. Have I not commanded you? Be strong and of good courage; do not be afraid or dismayed, for the Lord your God is with you wherever you go. Do not hide in the praise and worship but step into it as the pool at Bethsaida as the waters are stirred. Witness and experience God's healing and deliverance as His word washes our soiled and stained souls. No different than what God did for Elijah in destroying and annihilating Jezebel from the face of the earth so will He do for you and me, when we stop running and hiding from those people, places, and things that threaten our lives.

Chapter 9

DON'T FORGET MY LAWS!

Proverbs 3:1, "My son do not forget My law, But let your heart keep my commands; (2) For the length of days and long life, And peace they will add to you."

Here we are in one of the worst times in history wherein we are attempting to live through the coronavirus pandemic and its aftermath; Covid-19. If this was a movie it would be our modern-day version of "The Day, the Earth Stood Still." This virus had initially put the earth on pause. Covid traveled the world and leveled its fury against millions of people, leaving in its path of destruction hundreds of thousands dead and those numbers are on the rise. After two years of its existence, the constant increase in positive cases has overwhelmed our medical field, leaving our country vulnerable and in constant need of supplies. Covid 19's initial impact left our medical workers overworked and severely exposed to this deadly virus. But now the effects of being overworked have flooded all vocations and arenas of life. With that said, we have seen some areas or semblance of recovery, but Covid-19 has stumped us. There were at one point record numbers of job losses, but now we are faced with a market that is flooded with a record number of job openings that cannot be filled. Initially, I wondered why we cannot fill these jobs. And it is easy to say that people are being lazy and want to freeload of the stimulus checks and unemployment benefits. But has anyone ever considered that those millions of lives that were lost to Covid-19 coupled with the deaths of natural causes and other ailments, have created this vacuum wherein we cannot fill these job openings? I never would have imagined seeing days and times such as these in my lifetime. What has become somewhat unnerving is the impact that this pandemic has had on life period. We have lost so much of who we are as people and our ability to love and care for one another. This pandemic and its effects have caused a great depression among people, not economically but spiritually and mentally. It has choked the life out of so many people who were once lively but now simply exist as though they are zombies. God tells us to remember His laws because they will add the length of days - giving us long life and peace. Why would God tell us not to forget His laws? It is because when storms clouds rise and floods rush in it is easy to be overtaken; to lose oneself in the confusion and be driven to depression. Do not forget My laws because in them is long life and peace.

I can certainly understand why God would command us not to forget His laws. At the beginning of the pandemic, there was a bone-chilling and eerie moment for me on the morning of April 2, 2020. I was walking past the television at my job which was tuned in to CNN and they were breaking the news that the Pentagon had just ordered 100,000 body bags in anticipation of the death toll rising because of this virus. It shook me! It was a surreal moment and mind-boggling to the point where I beg the question as to why our leaders would lie and downplay the deadly potential of this virus and its path of destruction. For the life of me, I could not understand the arrogance and pompous attitudes of number 45 to think that he was invincible, and to allow his false sense of invincibility to overshadow the needs of our country. As the world was dying rapidly, all kinds of thoughts began to flood my mind. Thoughts of whether we are going to make it out of this and who would survive it? I did not want to lose my family and friends; and neither did I want to lose my life. Fear, apprehension, and doubt were creeping in all over the world.

The world was glued to the TV, watching and listening to horror reports. Reports of funeral home ordering freezer trailers to preserve bodies because they could not keep up with the death toll. Mass graves were dug, and bodies were burned in other countries. Hopelessness was consuming the earth. Do not forget My laws – they will add long life and peace to you. God always wants to remind us that He has the final say.

As I had been teaching bible study each morning at 6:00 am on Facebook live the scripture listed at the beginning of this chapter was the focus from March 30th thru April 2nd. The message rang aloud - do not for my laws. I believe in my heart that God was screaming this to me because regardless of what we were faced with from this pandemic to any other situation, God's law has promises that will keep us in the midst of our storms, pandemics, and all other conditions. When we keep the law of God, we find peace through our Lord and Savior Jesus Christ. Proverbs 3:1-19 cries out to us that wisdom is the principal thing and its worth and value far surpass anything we can possess or obtain. It is paramount that we engage God's word and obtain wisdom not to maintain through life but to prosper in it and triumph over the snares, snags, and stumps that beset us. We are the new creation of Christ Jesus - though we may lose in one area we gain in others to the glory of God. The word of God is our road map and navigator. Through it, we are front-loaded with God's grace and mercy all the days of life that we do not quit but remain resilient when everything around us has failed.

Chapter 10

1001 REASONS

I don't have enough fingers or toes combined to count the number of reasons and/or excuses that I can come up with to justify the need to quit life, dreams, goals, and desires; this has become one of the easiest things to do for so many people. It is not uncommon to hear these words "I don't have to accept that or take this, I'll just quit" and unfortunately that is a part of our new norm today. Everyone appears to be comforted by the fact that simply quitting is the answer when it's not. In fact, this outlook on life has caused many people to lose their fight and will to be more than conquerors and victors in life versus victims. When people quit, they become the victims of their own self-sabotage while blaming others for their unwillingness or inability to stay in the fight. What's worse is the fact that many people never take into consideration how many opportunities are missed to grow mentally tough when we fight through the quits. Take a moment to examine yourself and be honest through this process and look at what you have allowed psychologically to become a part of your norm, i.e. complaining about everything, life's not fair, nothing ever works in my favor, people are always working against me, and impoverished thoughts and the list are never-ending. Maybe some or none of these things are a part of your everyday outlook but what is? Whatever you come up with as your outlook, if it is unsatisfactory or negatively navigating you in the wrong direction then do something to change course. When we take a hard look within, we will find at the core of our self-examination the reason why we are where we are. Thinking about this, I am reminded of a couple of passages of scriptures in the bible where the Apostle Paul is encouraging and admonishing young Timothy during his time of adversity, weakness, and discouragement. The Apostle Paul must redirect Timothy's outlook and defeatist attitude or else he will miss out on the blessing of the Lord. The Apostle uses what was meant for Timothy's evil to work out for his good. Paul writes - **2 Timothy 3:16** *"All scripture is given by inspiration of God, and is profitable for doctrine, for reproof, for correction, for instruction in righteousness, that the man of God may be complete, thoroughly equipped for every good work."* This is to remind Timothy that he is completely and thoroughly equipped in Christ Jesus. In simple you can do this is what Paul was telling him. The Apostle Paul never said it would be easy or that doubt would not be a part of the process; but he did say you are thoroughly equipped. God had well supplied him as He does us through Christ Jesus to walk in power and authority and follow Him. Paul would have never left Timothy in charge of a church if he did not believe that he could handle it. Handle what? The criticism, challenges, and opposition from others who questioned his calling, readiness, leadership, strength, experience, and everything else people could find fault with. No different than Timothy, you must know that you can handle whatever comes your way. Because challenges and criticisms of your very being, will be called into question every day of your life; and being thin-skinned just will not do. Life is comprised of hurdles, obstacles, and people's messiness. And if you are thin-skinned, they will cause you and everyone else to contemplate giving up or quitting when the road becomes tough. Paul catches Timothy right out of the gate of despair by appealing to his foundation and upbringing. Paul reaches deep with the word of God which separate bone and marrow, writing - **2 Timothy 1:5-7,** *"when I call to remembrances the genuine faith that is in you, which dwelt first in your grandmother Lois and your mother Eunice, and I am persuaded is in you also. Therefore, I remind you to stir up the gift of God which is in you through the laying on of my hands. For God has not given us the Spirit of fear, but of power, love and a sound* *mind."* I know Timothy had to be blown because there was no excuse, rhyme, or reason he could give to remain in that low state or to allow adversity to cause him to come up short of God's glory. I know when he reflected on his life and the things, he witnessed in his mother and grandmother, he had no choice but to lift his voice and praise God. I know he was able to draw strength from his praise and worship. In fact, most of us are in that very same boat when we look back over our lives, we are without excuse as to why we cannot be more than conquerors in Christ Jesus; and pray, praise, and worship God through the storms of life.

As stated earlier there are 1001 reasons and excuses as to why we should quit and give up when things become tough or when the road, we are taking has been less traveled. But there is always one reason that is greater to stay in the fight than the 1001 reason you may come up with to get out and quit. That reason is you. I know you were thinking I was going to say Jesus Christ and He is the ultimate reason, but the reason is you, you trump any excuses and/or reasons you can find or come up with to quit or give up on what you are setting out to do or accomplish in life. If this was not so, Christ would not have died for you. **1 John 4:4 says, *"You are of God, little children, and have overcome them, because He who is in you, is greater than he who is in the world*.**" Who is He who dwells in us? Christ is He and His desires to make His home with us, and we are equipped thoroughly because of the Holy Spirit Who also dwells within us. My Lord! Our esteem should be high, and our outlook should encapsulate us standing on top of the world, hands raised high as we take in the breath of life with exhales of greatness, success, prosperity, accomplishments, triumphal and victorious shouts. I have to say again, My Lord! As I take into thought these four simple yet powerful words of **1 John 4:4,** **"*You are of God*"** - the thought, the meaning and implications that you are of God – simply put, you are derived from God. We can trace our origins or source to the author and giver of life, to His power and authority. And we have been given the Holy Spirit, who is a Spirit of power, love, and a sound mind. So, at no point in our lives should we ever feel inadequate, abandoned, or be in doubt about who we are and whose we are. Never again should we abandon our position, our lives, or our givens from God. And if that day should arise that you begin to doubt or entertain thoughts that weaken the soul and spirit of a person, which I'm sure will crop up from time to time, then immediately cast down those imaginations and every thought that exalts itself up against the will of God for your life (2 Corinthians 10:36) you entertain that mess and it drags you down the road of misery, anguish and the likes. Now encourage yourself in the Lord (1 Samul 30:6) and stop waiting for others or some good thing to happen before you are happy. Choose happiness and make something good happen and stop waiting on the happening of something good. With God, your potential and the possibilities are limitless. Therefore, tap into and use those gifts and talents that God has bestowed upon you for every good work.

Chapter 11

THERE IS MUCH TO THINK ABOUT!

Between the pandemic of 2020, covid-19, to the civil unrest of George Floyd's death, the year 2020, has presented us with much to think about and a lot to be considered. Never in my wildest dreams would I have imagined these days in my lifetime. Certainly, anything can happen and that is understood but to experience these two major events together is like the perfect storm. Think about it, in three to four months of covid 19's onslaught, 40,000,000 jobs were gone, 190,000 lives were lost, and the numbers were rising. Now add the protest coupled with civil unrest over George Floyd's death That have sparked national and international movements which have rocked our nation. Finally, to add insult to injury we had a president whose behaviors, actions, tweets, constant antagonizing rhetoric, divisiveness, racist overtones, lack of love, and empathy have seared the conscience of America. And no favors were done in the healing department for blacks in America when a photo appeared on Twitter comparing the resemblance between that one polarizing figure named Adolf Hitler and Donald Trump, which has flipped our cozy convenient country upside down. I am sure whoever assembled these pictures side by side on Twitter certainly had a bone to pick with the Trump administration as well as expressing their pain and emotional distraught with such a person.

As far as our nation being cozy, comfortable, and convenient, well, that is me being facetious

and overstating the truth. Do not get me wrong because I would not want to live in any other country than the United States because there are many pluses here but that does not minimize the fact that, as an African American man, cozy and convenience have never been an option for me or any other black person here in the United States of America. And those blacks who are cozying up to former President Donald Trump and have praised this narcissist and demigod ways have a rude awakening ahead of them. It is like the old joke of when a young boy and a snake were at the top of a mountain and the snake asked the young man to take him down the mountain with him; and the snake promised not to bite him. So, the young man with some apprehension put the snake in his pocket and scaled down the mountain. When the young man reached the bottom, he put his hand in his pocket to pull out the snake, and the snake bit him. The young man shocked and hurt, asked the snake why did you bite me after promising not to do so? And the snake replied because I am a snake. In a similar fashion, Donald Trump whom I am not calling a snake but shares values using people for his benefit; and like clockwork, you will feel the bite of his mistrust. He has been faithful and consistent in this department, as some of his former constituents, colleagues, cabinet members, and family who has committed their lives to help this selfish and crude person - and still, he bites them. Our country has been divided as he has spewed hatred and lies repeatedly. It is unbelievable to see how many Christians have been lullabied to sleep by his rhetoric and self-proclamation of being the chosen one while pointing to the sky. God does not choose people like this to honor His name and claim that he has done more for Christians than Jesus. With all that said, let me jump off this soap box. This is not the land of the Free and Brave. Yes, there are so many people who have laid down their lives for our country to strive for this dream of freedom and equality for all. But there are so many cowards who are full of hatred, deceitfulness, and cunning craftiness that hide behind white privilege. It is in this land of systemic racism that these people have raised their head to new heights and deeper depths. Our country is in civil unrest and a war is ensuing whose combatants are made up of several different entities and factions. It is crazy to think we are where we are as a nation, we could be so much better. I fear for my kids who are growing up in such a time as this. My only comfort is in Christ Jesus who reigns, and I know that He has our lives in His hands. Please do not mistake my thoughts; I love all people and have friends whom I consider my brothers and sister that are white and of other ethnicities. But this country has been forever cloaked in hoods and sheets and that is tragic. Life has been a struggle and with these other issues at play the struggles have been compounded; and that is a reality. These very struggles can leave you feeling helpless and hopeless. Therefore, with all that is happening, it is important for us to gear up our minds with thoughts that are positive and reaffirm our commitment to succeed and overcome the challenges of life. Thoughts that align with God's word and not those that are negative which causes us to drift away to nothing. Negative thoughts narrow our vision and willfulness to succeed. Thoughts that are birthed out of scripture are what is needed to fortify us as we battle the quits. Just so that I am clear on the meaning of battling the quits, it is waging war internally against those thoughts, emotions, and feelings that drives one to quit. As for me, those thoughts of quitting on life are no longer an option and never Will be as long as Jesus Christ is Lord and that is forever. But as stated earlier in another chapter, I have had my days of quitting and giving up on my dreams, goals, and desires because of struggle and adversity. Those days are long gone, and I no longer sit at that table feeding myself thoughts that impede or destroy my future. I have the Lord to thank for this. As for those who do not share my sentiments or enthusiasm to excel, it is easy to be pushed into that mindset of giving up and quiting. We need to be rooted in the good fight of faith and persevere through those storms.

In the book of 2 Timothy, chapter 3, verse 14, the Apostle Paul encourages Timothy who is in a struggle and faced with several storms, to "...continue in the things which you have learned and been assured of, …". a couple of different storms that are challenging and difficult. The Apostle Paul tells him this "***...continue in the things which you have learned and have been assured of, …***". Now history gives us some insight as to Timothy's troubles and discouragement, but one can never know the gravity of it without being there to experience it for Themselves. However, the Apostle Paul gave Timothy some excellent advice. No different we as Christians have the benefit of the bible which answers our problems but like most individuals when trouble comes knocking at our doors, we become shipwrecked, faint, and lost at sea. When the Apostle Paul says, "You continue in the things which you have learned and are assured of, this does several things for us. First, it builds our faith to trust in the Lord our God, and to stand on the knowledge we have acquired through the word of God. Second, it causes us to act on that information thus leading us to become wise and diligent. And finally, we will develop discretion which is the freedom to decide without the pressures of life and others impacting our decisions. So, battle the quits by fortifying yourself with what you have acquired from the word of God; and believe that you can achieve and do anything you want once you set your mind to do so. Remember you can do all things through Christ Jesus who strengthens you (Phil 4:13). But it is up to you to believe that you can in Christ Jesus.

Chapter 12

DEALING WITH MY REALITY

I started writing a book on this chapter alone called dealing with my reality. After completing three chapters, I thought it over and contemplated whether I should continue writing the book or add it as a chapter to this one. As you can see, I concluded that it would be better to add it to this book and keep it moving. This chapter deals with my time in quarantine when I was diagnosed with covid-19. It was Sunday, August 02, 2020, the day after my mom's birthday – God rest her soul. It was one of the most chilling points in my life that being literal and metaphorical. Late that Sunday morning it felt as though I was coming down with a sickness like a sinus infection or a cold – so I told my wife if this continued into the next morning that I would call in to work and to my medical provider and that is exactly what I did Monday morning. By the time I spoke with my doctor via video visit Monday afternoon, I was already feeling better even though I still went in to be tested for covid-19. The initial symptoms had kind of blown over like a brief storm passing through but by Tuesday morning a new wave of symptoms came knocking at my door. At this point, I kinda knew but was not sure if I had covid-19. When those symptoms came it was like a surprise party when they all showed up at once. The unwanted guests were shortness of breath, coughing, loss of smell, and diarrhea. With all this starting to occur, I went on and self-quarantined in the basement because I wanted to take the necessary precautions to minimize the risk of my family catching this mess. However, with all this going on the reality of being infected with this virus did not set in until I received that call on Wednesday afternoon. I was asked "Is this Mr. Stubblefield?" I replied, "Yes, it is." She went further to ask, "Has anyone contacted you yet?" I replied, "No ma'am." Then she said, "Well, this is Kaiser Permanente and I want to advise you that you have Covid-19." It was as though someone had just dropped a bomb on me. My mind went sailing immediately and it traveled to every Covid-19 port of call and/or destination that existed. Places like the Island of Death, Respirator Isles, the land of no return, suffering city, and the list goes on. For a minute I was lost, shaken and devastated. I called my wife and children. Everyone had to immediately leave their jobs and quarantine for the next 14 days. Of course, they all had to be tested and this was life-changing. Mind you this was pre-vaccination and covid was in its initial wave in the United States and no one had any real answers to this monster sweeping the nation.

Not knowing what lies ahead, I called my sister to inform her, and she began crying and so did I. This virus was a known killer. At the point I had contracted it, it had already consumed 160,000 lives and counting. In fact, the infection rate and death toll were on a rapid increase United States-wide. I became so overwhelmed with it and its range of possibilities, I called my assistant Pastor who also happens to be one of my best friends, and started planning to have my personal and confidential information transferred to him in case this thing had gotten the best of me. In doing so, this would minimize my wife having to grapple with my sudden demise while attempting to figure everything else out. This is how fast your life changes when you are dealing with something that has the possibility of consuming you in days. It is funny now that I have come through it. But at that moment, the battle had just begun, and I was already surrendering. That is how fast you mentally decline when you are told this is your lot; Covid-19; again, this was before they had a vaccination. Oddly enough, those unexpected guests (symptoms) who showed up immediately began to dissipate just as quickly as they came. When I received that call that I was positive for Covid-19 that Wednesday morning, the shortness of breath, the cough, and diarrhea had left. The only thing that was remaining was the loss of smell and a little weakness. By Thursday evening, August 06, I was feeling great, and I had some workout equipment sent to the basement by my son. Immediately, I jumped into a full 30-minute-high intensity circuit training program; which was not wise at all. It was as though nothing had ever happened to me. But this was just the beginning of my trial. Physically I felt I was good but not mentally. The truth of the matter is this virus is tricky because no sooner than the symptoms left some other things could have shown up just as quickly. Praise the Lord they did not but I have heard it happen to others who had covid-19. Just when they thought they had cleared the last hurdle out of nowhere the virus resurfaced with new challenges. But again, praise the Lord that it did not happen to me. I bless the Lord because I know personally of some who struggled but recovered; and I have a couple of friends who did not make it.

As stated, I pretty much cleared the physical hurdles in the first week of my diagnosis. In fact, my physical symptoms had disappeared within days of experiencing them with exception of the loss of smell. But mentally the battle had just begun. I was entering into another battle round. You talk about battling the quits. It's one thing to self-quarantine but in the famous words of my mother "it is a horse of another color" when it is mandatory. In the first several days, my basement, which initially appeared to be nice in size, suddenly began to close in on me. Looking ahead, two weeks appeared to be a lifetime. Yes, I was only quarantined to the basement. But when you are quarantined inside of a quarantine it becomes stressful. The other part of my mental fight was for my family. They were all tested immediately, and the results were negative but that did not mean the virus would not show up in the days ahead. That is why they had to quarantine for fourteen days. I could not shake the thoughts of the possibilities of my family getting this awful virus because of me and what the impact could be especially for my wife who has had underline health issues. My job is to protect my family, and, in this instance, this was something beyond my reach. Only one person could handle this, and his name is Jesus Christ. I kept praying to the Lord to get us through this season unbattered and He did just that. Outside of worrying about them, I had temporarily reached a dark moment. I kept thinking to myself, "what if I do not wake up the next morning what is this virus going to do to me?" Battling these thoughts is something else. These thoughts get you into the mindset of woe is me. They have you checked out while you are still checked in. Listen, I believe that I am heaven bound but I still want to spend time with my family and see my grandchildren. I still wanted to live life to its fullest and enjoy the days ahead with my wife. Yes, I still wanted to preach the gospel of Jesus Christ and see brighter days. Everything appeared bleak for a short moment in time. I was fighting within trying to free myself of all these doom and gloomy thoughts. This is what Satan wants from us; and that is to give up living and throw in the towel. Looking at CNN and seeing the number of cases and death totals rise was frightening. I knew I was among those statics of confirmed cases, but would I eventually become one of those statistics that resulted in death? I was shaking for a moment until one night I was listening to the gospel music station on Direct TV. Oh my gosh! That old song from gospel artist Fred Hammond, "Your Steps Are Ordered" played and it was like Jesus was speaking directly to me. As soon as I finished listening to it I looked it up on my phone to add to my playlist then his other songs popped up - "No Weapon", "Jesus is All", and "Just To Be Close To You". I felt that I was winning at that moment as I was cracking open my bible and coming upon the checkered flag. That race was over, and I was about to take my victory lap - praise the Lord!

Like clockwork, the Virginia Department of Health contacted me daily via phone or text to track my symptoms and my family's progress. One representative said I was fortunate to be as healthy as I was because it was key to getting me through this as easily as I did. I agreed, however, I told her about the true factor in this was Jesus Christ and I firmly believed that; and she agreed. This is how awesome God is. Back in March 2020, when covid-19 had started to settle into the United States and ravage the lives of people; God had told me to increase and strengthen myself cardio vascularly. At that point, I shared with my wife what the Lord had told me to do. Honestly, I thought He had told me this as a preventive maintenance to contracting the virus. Mind you, I was already working out, but the Lord wanted me to intensify my training and that I did. What is amazing about all this, is the fact six months prior to all this I was having a very difficult time running or jogging because of sports injuries and age. It was painful and I could barely squeeze out a mile before giving in. So, I was training at Planet Fitness on the ellipticals two to three times a week. But like everything else the gyms had started closing due to the pandemic and social distances. We were in a lockdown nationwide. It was at this moment that God had begun strengthening my legs to run and the knee pains had diminished to the point of almost being nonexistent. I started running and running I did. Fast forward, some four months later I tested positive for covid-19 and its impact on my life was minimal in comparison to many others whose lives have been taken or severely impacted physically. Again, I thank the Lord for bringing me through and preparing me physically to bare this virus. A couple of days removed from quarantine, nervously I decided to take a run. There was some fear of being exposed to the virus again, so I ran with a vented running mask that I had ordered from Amazon. I experienced some leg fatigue as though I was not getting enough oxygen, but I was able to muster out three miles. Here I am a month after my quarantine and I'm running weekly three to five miles three to four times a week with relative ease. God is amazing, I am thankful and blessed. All I can tell you is that when the hour seems darkest in your life to battle the quits. Don't give up or in, because that is the easiest thing to do. With God on your side all things are possible through Christ Jesus who strengthens you. When these moments seem as though the end is nearing for you – it's just the beginning for God. So, hold on and strap in, because God is about to take you on an adventure and journey that no one else can.

Chapter 13

IT'S BEEN A LONG ROAD

It has been hard, it has been difficult, it has been a long road, and it has been a 30-plus year journey with the Alexandria Sheriff's Office; and make no bones about it, there have been many good days and equally, there have been those that were bad. I often think about those days when I remained silent when I should have spoken up and spoken up when I should have remained silent. In this thirty-plus year journey there are two different seasons of my life wherein I left the Sheriff's Office and was asked to come back, and on both occasions I did. I often imagine where I would be had I not left for the simple fact that my 30-year retirement would have been September 13, 2019. Only God truly knows but I am sure I would be home alongside other retirees who were before and after me enjoying my reward; however, with that said my retirement (reward) is temporarily delayed but not denied. It is now November 2021, and we are in the midst of a pandemic, Covid-19. It's been over a year since we entered the pandemic, and we are attempting to grapple with it as it has mutated, and a second strand is plaguing the country. There is a second pandemic running alongside the first whose origins are rooted in police brutality and systemic racism. To add to boot, a former President recently removed from office who is a narcissist that drum-majored the divide in this country and dragged it through the mud. There is a lot more to be said about all of this but that is for another day, another time, or perhaps what so many others are doing, another book. With all that said, I have found myself battling with quitting and moving on from the Sheriff's Office. To be honest, I am immersed in the thoughts, and surrounded by its stench which sickens and poisons me. Pitting the unsettling urges to quit and walk away. There are so many good reasons to do so but not many valid ones.

My career has been faced with adversities and challenges all of which have worked out for me in one way or another. As I briefly reminisce, I can remember early in my career when I was new to the Office and no one wanted to partner with me because I was a native of Alexandria; and of course, the jail was full of Alexandrians from my community. So, staff did not trust me to do my job without hesitation. Those were some difficult but short-lived days. Their gross mischaracterization of judgment had completely missed its mark. My friends who were incarcerated respected my choices in life and who I was as a person and looked out for me. They kept me in the know of everything that was happening in the jail which kept me looking good in the eyes of the Office. Boy did the tides turn. Now everyone wants to work alongside me and ride this wave. Those were awesome days leading to me receiving honors of the employee of the year, WTOP's Unsung Hero honors of the 3rd quarter – being interviewed by Cathy Hughes; Sheriff's Office employee of the quarter, and a host of other honors. These were some good ole days and I loved them. Of course with good days also come challenges. With challenges are those accompanying thoughts of wanting to quit but I ignored those emotions for the most part.

Another challenging moment occurred one evening when I left my home around midnight driving through the city when I noticed I was being followed by the Alexandria Police. I knew why they were tailing me, but I continued and played along with this Tom Foolery. They did not recognize who I was but simply homed in on the fact that I was a young black male driving a nice car. We were at the height of the gangs and drugs epidemic in the Washington Metropolitan Area; and yes, I fit their narrative and they thought they had one. After pulling me over on a trumped-up traffic violation, I displayed my Sheriff credentials and boy did they make a beeline back to their cruiser as though they had seen a ghost. It was laughable at first to see them tuck tail and run, but at that moment I did not recognize the ugliness of this systemic racism. After exposing the incident, which was buried, the very same Officer who was involved threatened to put a gun to my head the next time he pulled me over. This was the light end of the verbal exchange; but there would be no next time. He kept his distance and so did I. This incident coupled with some other racial incident was enough to cause anyone to quit but I did not give into my emotions at the time and thank God I did not.

Fast forwarding some 30 years later, I find myself in the Sheriff's Office yet grappling with one of several dilemmas on a different scale in this different season of time. I am tossed in what direction I take and what decisions I make. My concern is weighty wherein I left the Sheriff's Office on two different occasions with no intention of returning as an employee. Young and ignorant, I did not consider or realize the repercussions or consequences of my decision. The adverse impact of using my retirement to live off was incredibly dumb. Hindsight, I should have found some other stream of income to live off while building a company on the first occasion and some other stream of income while serving in ministry the second time around. So now I must either wait for six more years before retiring to receive a halfway decent retirement check or find something else that will offset the loss if I walk away now. In any event, I am in struggle because I do not want to make a fool's mistake. There are several battles that rage within. I am prepared to stay and to leave. I know I am gifted and talented and have much to offer; I know I can make a difference in the Sheriff's office. But somewhere along life's highway, I became an invisible man. Yes, they see me, but they don't. They look through and/or pass me daily and it hurts especially when you consider my contributions to the Sheriff's office. Unfortunately, my labor appears to be in vain – they have only led to the verbiage of a good job but not to promotion. And when I think about some who have been promoted over me, they are by no means bad people or candidates for promotion, but I should have been promoted before some of them.

My reason for saying this is simple. They do not have my experience or my contributions, and neither do they have my tenure. I am not downing these individuals, but I simply note a fact and it is undeniable; and my work ethics and evaluations speak for themselves. Lord, I know that they see me because of Your wonderful work done in and through me. But for some reason, their eyes are heavy with scales that veil my presence. Now could this be You Lord shielding me from that which is unseen and destroys? Or is this the devil's discouragement? His attempts to destroy and empty me of that which pertains to You. There is a war waging eternally, a battle fighting the quits. One thing is for sure, I will not be that angry and disgruntled person. God has simply been too amazing to me, and my family and I must be thankful even in this. Though I feel like it I will not be a quitter, and neither should you when it appears that you are invisible. God sees us and promotion comes from Him when He knows we are ready.

I know I have so much to offer as a leader, as a senior deputy, and as a chaplain that can aid in the growth and afford development of others, and I cannot afford to throw that away because of my emotions and feelings. Feelings aside there is much work to do for Lord. Therefore, I must adhere to Colossians 3:17, "*And whatever you do in word or deed, do all in the name of the Lord Jesus, giving thanks to God the Father through Him.*" Now, who in their right Christian mind can quit and then in the same breath give thanks to God in Christ? Again, we cannot make quitting our go-to plan whenever something is not going our way. We have to always battle the quits, read God's word, and give God the glory for all that He has done and is doing in our lives.

Chapter 14

TRAINING TO QUIT

Who in the world trains to quit? I do not know of anyone who does such a thing and certainly, I know I do not; but there may be some who do and for what reasons I cannot give; however, it happens wherein people have trained long and hard and then quit because they hit a bump in the road. I know this is an oxymoron to think that someone trains to quit. Especially after dedicating their time, energy, and effort to being successful or achieving their goals and the individual simply quit. What is training and why is it so important to do so? Training is the education, instruction, or discipline of a person setting out to accomplish or achieve a goal. Training is an intended process to transition a person from one level to level up to the next. It can be a rigorous process to ready and equip a person for the journey that lies ahead in order that one may endure unexpected challenges and adversities. On the flip side of things, it can be as simple as enlightening someone with a few additional steps to a process to make someone more efficient.

Thinking back to high school like so many other kids I had a dream, a goal, and a desire for what I wanted to be in life. I dreamt about my future. Some of those dreams, goals, and desires were short in nature while others were long-term. Speaking of which, I can remember my sophomore and junior years at TC Williams High School, I played JV football, and we had two great seasons. But to level up to varsity for my senior season I had to prepare because the competition to play at wide receiver was great. I can remember training in the spring of my junior year and throughout that entire summer. I would always drive down to my friend's house, Reginald Howell, who was one of our backup quarterbacks to train. I was a wide receiver, and the odds were against me, as I had my eyes set on receiving a football scholarship from any school that would have me. The reason why I said the odds were against me were for a couple of reasons. First of which, our team was stacked with talented and outstanding players, and second of which, I was not one of Coach Furman's favorite players. He liked me as a person, but he did not see a future for me as a player beyond high school. As he told my sister during my junior year when she asked him at the college fair, did he think I would receive a football scholarship? Without cracking a smile, he said no and that was the end of that conversation. With that said, I knew I had to work hard in hope that someone would see me and my potential. So, when I was not training with Reggie, running route patterns, and sprinting the football field at GW Junior High School, I was often found running four to five miles throughout the city, sprinting hills, and doing calisthenics to get faster and stronger. I would often imagine myself playing in the NFL, burning defensive backs and scoring touchdowns. I could hear my name being cheered on by the fans; and each time I saw myself and heard them, I trained harder to reach that place. I could taste and smell it. It was every bit as real to me as breathing. But I had to get through the process and that began with having a strong senior season and then being offered a scholarship and that is what happened. Now with that said, I could have found every excuse to quit. No, my father was not in my life, he and my mother divorced when I was younger and in 9th grade, he passed. No, I did not have any older siblings who played sports. My older sister was very supportive and so was my mom; but their understanding of playing and training for the game was limited. So, I had to go for what little I knew.

Back to getting that scholarship, I was not the named starter my senior year although I had two stellar seasons at the JV level. My man Chucky Grimes was, but I played like I was the starter and hoped someday that my name would be called among them, but that never happened. But I did receive a football scholarship no thanks to Furman who in fact did not inform me that there were colleges interested in me. It was my friend, Shawn McNeil, who went to the coach's office to pick up his letters from universities interested in him, when he noticed other letters sticking out from underneath the yellow pages (phonebook) and pulled them out which had my name on them. He brought those letters to me. Otherwise, I would not have ever known any school was even remotely interested in me. With all that said, Mr. John Carr, spoke up for me one day at the regional final championships game against Pulaski County High School. Looking back, I believe God set it up, that Mr. Carr would happen to be sitting next to the Virginia Union Football Team scouts. He pointed me out to them; and that is how I ended up receiving an official offer to play football at Virginia Union University.

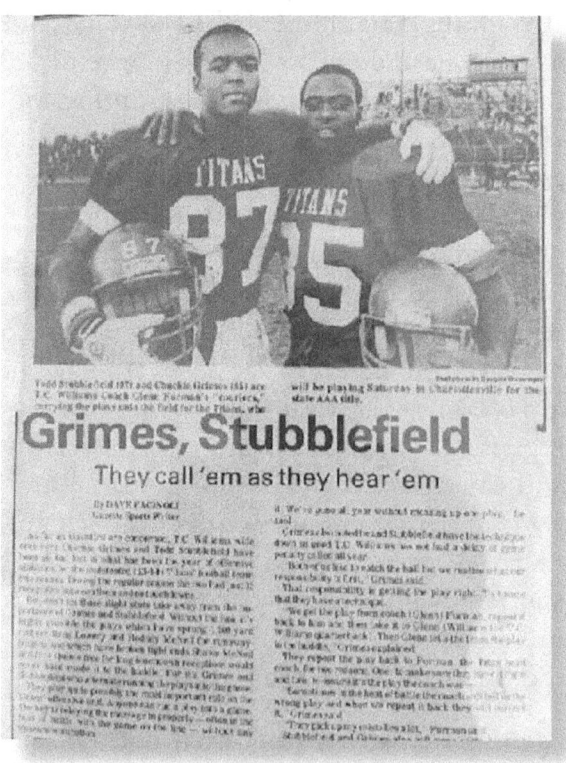

Todd Stubblefield (87) and Chuckie Grimes (85) are T.C. Williams Coach Glenn Furman's "couriers," carrying the plays onto the field for the Titans, who will be playing Saturday in Charlottesville for the state AAA title.

Grimes, Stubblefield

They call 'em as they hear 'em

By DAVE EAGNOLI
Gazette Sports Writer

Four more T.C. Williams High School football players have received college football scholarships. From left to right are on the front row are Sidney Ellis, Carlton Hallums, Todd Stubblefield and Rodney McNeil. Back left is T.C. Williams head Coach Glenn Furman right is James McNeil, Rodney's father.

Four more Titans earn college scholarships

By DAVE FACINOLI
Gazette Sports Writer

Four more players off the T.C. Williams High School Virginia AAA

Academy, center Mike Porterfield is expected to get a crew scholarship and quarterback Glenn Williams has agreed to attend Holy Cross on a basketball scholarship.

Earlier, runningback Bren Lowery

felt was the most potent offensive backfield Northern Virginia has ever seen. The two galloped through defenses all year long — at times it seemed with relative ease. Unfortunately McNeil, who averaged 8.4

totals showed 11 for the 1 However, his main role w blocker for Lowery and Mc addition he, along with (Grimes, alternated carr plays into the game — "fl according to Furman.

My training paid off. I was in a good place having been offered a scholarship and I was looking forward to the next level. Once I arrived at VUU, I was in tip-top shape. I was in the mindset of that oldie but goodie song by McFadden & Whitehead, "Ain't No Stoppin Us Now". Training had become the norm for me. I had been in a routine that had prepared and escorted me straight out of high school into my fresh-year college football training camp – those hard and painful practices of two and three times a day. In fact, sometimes before or after practice at Union, I would run about four to six miles like it was nothing and still had the energy to practice hard. But all this would be short-lived. I was injured in a freak hit during practice when my knee blew up like a balloon. Redshirted for the season, I did what I knew best and that was to train; and training is what I did; and because of my training, I healed quickly and prepared for the spring season. I do not know if Carl Bland remembers me, but he was a former VUU Panther who was at that time playing for Detroit Lions as a wide receiver. He was home from the season and had worked out with me in January of 86' giving me insight, training tips, and even some Detroit Lion's training gear. He made me a better receiver. I had an excellent spring season that year but at the end of it, I was cut by Coach Taylor. During the meeting, he invited me to return for my sophomore season and said if I made the travel squad, I would get my scholarship back. In my mind that would be easy because I was disciplined, determined, and focused. This was a minor challenge and setback in comparison to what it took to get there. Like the terminator I said I'll be back.

But something happened between the spring and the summer going into my sophomore season and what that was I have no idea; but I quit. I had trained hard during that period to get my scholarship back and was mentally prepared; but something clicked. Initially, I was determined to hurdle any obstacle placed before me to see my dreams come true, but I quit. I literally trained to quit. All my determination, discipline, and sweat equity mounted up to nothing more than to walk away from the game that I so loved. What in the world happened? Can someone explain it to me because I am still lost today some 30 years later as to what happened. I went back to school in my sophomore year but as a student and not as a student-athlete. Interestingly, Coach Taylor asked me to return to the team after the first one or two games of that season; because Donald Saunders who was playing receiver was injured during a game and I said no. I was angry with him for initially taking my scholarship and had lost my fight to excel and overcome the challenges. Without dragging this out any further, it all boiled down to me training only to end up quitting. In other words, all my training mounted up to quitting. This is where so many others are today and have been in their lives wherein, they have worked so hard to realize their dreams and then one day unexpectedly something snapped, and they simply quit and walked away. Everything they had worked so hard for went up in smoke and/or disappeared in the blink of an eye.

Quitting is not an event but a thought that leads to an attitude; and that attitude leads to an action, and that action defines one's character and our character becomes our norm. Today, I am still visited and haunted by that decision to quit. Yes, I have forgiven myself but thinking about the possibilities of where that road could have led to is what haunts me from time to time. But this was not the only dream I have given up on, since that time there have been many. And that is what I mean when I say quitting become your norm. Once you take this approach to life in various instances it will become a part of your character. The possibilities may have been great or may have amounted to nothing, but I will never know only God does. With all that said, do not let your training rewards or awards be a first-place quitter because you chose to give up and walk away. There are moments and times when there are no other options; but let those be your last resort and not become your initial thought. Battle the quits.

Chapter 15

SETTLING FOR BREADCRUMBS

Too often in life, we have settled for the breadcrumbs from the master's table instead of being persistent in pursuing the blessings, opportunities, and favors that await us; and that is a misfortune. Make no mistake, breadcrumbs are significant in that they offer some means of provision and sustenance for those in need. However, they are what remains and are leftover from something greater. And if breadcrumbs are all that you can get your hands on for the moment, that is fine but do not allow that to be your greater. We should never settle for the less, or the breadcrumbs if that is all we continue to come up with in our pursuit of whatever. No matter how many times that is all that we are afforded, we must know that if there is a remnant which is breadcrumbs, then there is a whole loaf to be had where crumbs have fallen from. The travesty in accepting breadcrumbs as a blessing is that psychologically it caps our growth and we stop striving for better. In other words, we have become accustomed to settling for less when there is so much more to be had.

Why settle for crumbs when we can have a slice of bread and eventually possess the entire loaf for ourselves? Matthew, Chapter 15, verses 21-28, provides us with an interesting and powerful exchange between Jesus and a woman from Canaan who recognizes the breadcrumb blessing but does not settle for them. It is important to note that this woman is not identified by name but by region, because it gives us some insight into her social and economic construct. If you will allow me this instance to build a foundation on this scripture without having any additional information; there are some things that we can safely assume.

The first of which is that she is a servant by trade, a servant by proxy, and/or a servant by default. By trade because her family's ancestorial heritage are generational servants because that was their lot in life due to their ancestor Ham's misdeeds. In Genesis, chapter 9, verse 22, Ham, the father of Canaan, saw his father's nakedness and exposed it to his brothers. When Noah awoke from his drunkenness to Ham's misdeeds, he cursed his descendants. Noah said in verse 25, *"Cursed be Canaan; A servant of servants He shall be to his brethren."* In many cases, people will not rise above what has been passed down to them from generation to generation or culture to culture. In fact, there are times when people will fall into certain professions or various forms of work because that is what their families have done for decades not realizing their own potential. So, they do what they are accustomed to seeing or knowing based on other family members, environment and/ or friends' choices and not their own. Man, the world is vast, and the opportunities are without measure. God has stored in each of us, His children, His Holy Spirit who is a treasure with untold, unimaginable, and invaluable riches. If we only knew our true worth. So many Christians miss the mark of life in that their understanding of Christ's death on the cross was salvation alone. Unfortunately, some people cannot see beyond the present status or conditions that have been passed down to them. Thus, hindering their potential and purpose. They will settle for what has been given or even expected of them though they have other dreams and desires. The Canaanite woman was a servant by proxy because they had little to no rights and was a servant of servants, based on the curse. Therefore, others who had the power would be their voice and/or representation in society leaving them at the mercy of someone else's will. And finally, she was a servant by default because she did not grow up with aspirations of being a servant but was thrust into that capacity because it was their curse.

What I love about this woman is that she refused to be denied her **blessings, not her rights**. In fact, this woman bucked the norm or status quo because she had no rights, the only thing she had was her faith and courage enough to use it despite all else. And her faith was more than enough for Jesus to change her conditions, status, and the situation in life. In fact, her faith was more than sufficient to change someone else's situation and conditions. This woman's faith allowed her to stand in the gap. That bridgeless space existed between her daughter and God. A note of fact, the bible does not record how old her daughter was as to whether she was a youth or an adult except that she was demon-possessed. Nevertheless, her mother did not accept her daughter's condition.

See, to battle the quits, we must have faith and courage enough to use our faith and stop settling for less. Too many times we give up before the battle begins and lose the fight without even giving ourselves the chance to win. Let us continue in this story. I cannot imagine what was going through the Canaanite woman's mind during her exchange with Jesus but what I do know is that she was not going to be denied her blessing; and neither should you. At her very first interaction with Jesus, she was ignored. Matthew 15: 22-23, says that she cried out to Him, but He answered her not. This is problem number one for most of us. Because when we are ignored, we not only take it personally which is a normal reaction, but we also allow that to be the catalyst for making bad decisions. I know in my past when I felt disrespected, I would tell others that I would not be disrespected and then simply quit.

It becomes worse when Jesus tells the Canaanite woman that it is not good to take the children's bread and throw it at the little dogs. What another disrespectful blow, but she strikes back with, yes Lord, even the little dogs eat the crumbs from their master's table. This woman was not going to be denied, because she was determined. Are you determined? Are you prepared to persevere and push past the roadblocks you encounter? You can do all things through Christ who strengthens you (Phil 4:13); but you must own this scripture and not simply allow it to be a familiar favorite quote. As I have already stated, stop quitting and start fighting for your dreams, goals, desires, and whatever else you want to see happen positively in your life. Again, perseverance, importunity, and determination are the tools of success and victory to our otherwise defeat. You are not defeated, but more than a conqueror in and through Christ Jesus our Lord and Savior.

Chapter 16

MY LATTER DAYS

Job 8:7 says, "Though your beginnings were small, yet your latter end would increase abundantly."

This scripture arises out of Jobs longing to die because of the mental anguish he was suffering from the loss of his children and possessions. In his eyes, life had turned quickly, and misfortune had come knocking at his door. God knows I cannot imagine the pain he must have been experiencing; and neither can I know the pain of others whose situations are like Job's. We all know or at least are, or even may be familiar with the story of Job and how he lost everything. It was nothing of his own doing that brought him to this tragic season in life; it was simply that the devil was seeking someone that he may devour. We see the situation unfold before our very eyes in Job 1:6-11, wherein Satan pops in on the sons of God who were in God's presence – and God asked Satan from where he has come. Satan responds going to and from throughout the earth. Satan was looking for an opportunity to devour someone; and God responds have you considered my servant Job? And from that moment on Job's life would be turned upside down. He would encounter a season that would have destroyed most people, from the loss of his material wealth to that of all his children shortly thereafter. Satan did a job on Job, as he has and continues to do on the lives of others today.

We all have a beginning, a starting place, and a point of reference that we can look back on as a reminder of whence we have come. A place that is a benchmark or a line of demarcation dividing two distinct areas of our lives, that which was, is, and/or is to come. Because looking back on my life I know there were times when I thought I was at my wick's end and there was no relief in sight. But looking back now, I cannot only point to the moment when my situations swung in a different direction, but I can praise God for them. These are those benchmarks and lines of demarcation when God will remind us of where we were and where He has brought us to. They are our changing points and times of illumination at our darkest hours. This is where our pain becomes those wings like eagles in Isaiah 40:31 and we mount up as we begin to mature, grow, and soar in life.

When Job's friend Bildad said to him in chapter 8, verses 5-7, "Though your beginnings was small, yet your latter end would increase abundantly" if Job would earnestly seek God and make his supplication to the Almighty; Bildad could not have imagined how profound a statement that was. It was not only true in Job instance but would be so for those to come and now it is for our lives today. With all that said, let us look at this from a personal perspective wherein our latter days will be better and more prosperous than our former days if we too seek God and make supplication to the Almighty.

Much like the devil himself, there are some people who will enter your life whose sole purpose is to be disruptive and destructive. I do not necessarily believe it is always intentional that some people are this way, but the devil will use whomever he can with intentions to devour you, your dreams, and /or your relationship with others and Christ Jesus. While writing this chapter there is a story that has grabbed national attention and is sad. Without mentioning her name this young lady committed suicide on January 31, 2022, by jumping out of the window of a high-rise building, whose life externally appeared to be on the rise of greatness. She was thirty years old, a college grad, and a lawyer. She was also a former Ms. North Carolina and Ms. USA winner. She was doing magnificent work locally and nationally and to the naked eye she appeared to be doing well. But for some odd reason, she thought it would be better to end her life that morning, which left her family distraught. She had touched and inspired the lives of many people through her life journey. But on the morning of her death, according to a report she tweeted one last message and it read – may this day bring you rest and peace. As I contemplated the message, I wondered what was possibly ailing and causing that much pain that she chose that end. I can only speculate why such a tragic end but like many others, I will never know the truth. But with speculation, I want to point out there are some people who will never mean you any good. There are some people who will never be happy with your success and accomplishments. There are some people who never want to see you grow or spread your wings. There are some people who will be jealous of you and will do whatever they can to derail you. There will be others who want to see you fail because their lives never amounted to anything. In the eyes of some, no matter how well you fair or high you soar you will never measure up. And at the end of the day, there will be those whose mission and enjoyment will be to cause you to quit and who will stop at nothing to see that you do. Whatever you do, do not quit. Yes, it is easier said than done in many instances, however, your latter days will be greater than your former days if you seek God and make supplication to the Almighty. Again, I cannot imagine what this young lady was experiencing and the pain of it all it, but whatever it was, she determined at that moment it was best for her and whomever the tweet was directed to end it all. My prayer for whoever is reading this book is that no matter where you find yourself in life, no situation is bigger than life or worth yours. Please know that God is bigger than your situation; and is the answer to all our problems. And if you cannot see God then reach out to someone who is professionally trained to assist in these matters. The thief comes to steal, and to kill and to destroy but Jesus came that we may have life, and it more abundantly. Who is the thief? It is anything, situation, or person who comes to rob you of your joy and your will to live. So, whatever you are battling for, do not forget to live and live life to the fullest.

Chapter 17

YOUR LACK CAN BECOME YOUR LIVING

2 Kings 4:3; *"Then he said, "Go borrow vessels from everywhere, from all your neighbors – empty vessels; do not gather just a few."*

Just reading this passage of scripture leaves me in such awe that I am having trouble finding a place to begin. There is so much to be said, and even more to glean from this scripture that I do not want to miss the opportunity to fill your spirit man with hope, encouragement, empowerment, and expectation. Awe yes! Let us begin with, I could not sleep. It was Friday, July 23, 2021, at approximately 1:30 am, and I was wrestling with finding a comfortable sleeping position. I had been dealing with what my doctor described as arthritis in my neck which was causing numbness in my fingertips and arm. So, I purchased a cervical pillow in an attempt to adjust to my sleeping posture. Without having any immediate relief, I found myself on my knees and praying about my pain and everything that came to my heart. In that prayer, I petition God for the increase that I may retire from the Alexandria Sheriff's Office by July 1st, 2022, if not earlier, and At this point, He laid this scripture of the widow and her two sons on my heart. As I continued to pray in the wee hours of the morning, the Lord laid to mind - can you imagine how great the widow's expectation was? She approached the Prophet Elisha with her husband, servant of Elisha, is dead, and the creditor was coming to take her two sons to be his slaves – which was lawful and customary. He asked her, "What shall I do for you? And what is in your house? She replied "Your maidservant has nothing in the house but a jar of oil. ***"Then he said, "Go borrow vessels from everywhere, from all your neighbors – empty vessels; do not gather just a few."*** If you are or are not familiar with the rest of this story, we will cover some of it shortly and I would encourage you to read it but for now, let us pause for a second and look at what the Lord had laid on my heart about expectation relating to this passage of scripture. As stated earlier I had been praying because I could not sleep in which I had asked God to supply all my needs and allow me to retire soon; and He brought me to this passage of scripture. All this widow had available to her was a jar of oil in the house, which was her only possession, yet her debt was so large that the creditor was coming to take her two sons as slaves. Now when she told Elish that, he instructed her to borrow empty vessels from all her neighbors and not just a few. Her expectation was so great, and she did what she was told. She asked no questions, and she pondered no thoughts, she went in the house as instructed after her sons began gathering vessels as many as they could borrow and brought them to her. She began to pour the oil. That little jar of oil poured until there were no more vessels to be filled. Amazingly, if there was an empty vessel, the oil would have continued to pour and fill each one. From that tiny jar of oil, God miraculously filled every vessel to the extent that her home was overflowing and supplied with all that she had need of. That is the wonder-working power of God. Whatever your jar of oil is or better yet whatever it is you have in your possession God is able to cause it to multiply, increase, enlarge, expand, and overflow you. The widow went back to Elisha, and he told her now go sell the oil and pay your debt and live off the rest. As I think about this, God increases this widow's net worth from nothing to a thriving oil business. Again, he said to her, sell the oil and live off the rest. God's richest according to His kingdom is unimaginable and without limitations. With that said, I am setting out to retire. My retirement package from the city of Alexandria will be small as things stand now because I broke service twice leaving the Sheriff's Office using my retirement to live. But now

I have great expectations from God to enlarge my territory and cause my retirement to pour as the oil did. I believe that God will take what I have and turn it into what I need to live off when I retire. I believe that my companies Spot Me and Suited Communications will become my greater. I am going to trust God and lean not to my own understanding but acknowledge Him in all my ways and He will direct my path (Proverbs 3:5-6). No different than God did for the widow He will also do for you and me.

But here is where God affirms His position in our lives today in meeting our needs. John 14: 12-14, "Most assuredly, I say to you, he who believes in Me, the work that I do he will do also; and greater works than these he will do, because I go to My Father. And whatever you ask in My name, that I will do, that the Father may be glorified in the Son. If you ask anything in my name I will do it." Luke 11:9, "So I say to you, ask, and it will be given to you; seek, and you will find; knock, and it will be open to you." And there are so many more scriptures that point to God's power meeting our needs. But this one scripture somewhat coincides with the widow and her sons (2 Kings4:3) in Mathew 14:13-21, when the disciples tell Jesus to send the people away so that they may go to the villages to find food for the hour is late. But Jesus tells the disciples, they do not need to go away, you give them something to eat. And they said to Him, "We have here five loaves of bread and two fish." Jesus said to bring them to Me. In essence, the bible said, Jesus took the five loaves and two fish and looked up to heaven, He blessed and broke and gave the loaves to the disciples and they fed the multitude which turned out to be 5000 men not including women and children. And they took up twelve baskets of the fragments that remained. So, God took what was little and made it much. This holds true and remains with everything that pertains to you and me, today.

Therefore, do not quit on your present conditions or give up because of your lack, but look up to heaven and bless what you have. By faith, God will take that which you have blessed and multiply it to meet your need and increase it so that your ending possession will be greater than your beginning possession. We must learn to set our minds on Christ and things above. In doing so we will not be distracted by that which is below. Therefore, do not let your desperation cause you to give up, battle the quits.

Chapter 18

WHO AM I?

Who am I, is the question that Moses asked God when he was assigned to lead this mass exodus out of Egypt. In Exodus 3:10, God says to Moses "Come now, therefore, and I will send you to Pharaoh, that you may bring My people, the children of Israel, out of Egypt. (11) But Moses said to God, who am I that I should go to Pharaoh and that I should bring the children of Israel out of Egypt?" I cannot imagine for the life of me the thoughts that may have crossed Moses's mind when God spoke to him about this larger-than-life undertaking. I am sure the thoughts were weighty because Moses did not hesitate to question his ability and God's choice to manage and handle such a task. Moses goes from this tucked away quiet and reserved life in the mountains caring for his father-in-law's sheep to God appearing to him one day out of a burning bush, saying in so many words, come now I am sending you back to the place you ran from to lead my people out of. Now I must say that there are times in our lives When we will run and hide. Those times when we will quit and give up but God will bring us back full circle to face that very thing. Think about it, some of the things you ran and hid from and never addressed are right back in your face. There is an adage, you can run but you cannot hide. I am sure this was very uncomfortable for Moses because at one point he was on Egypt's most wanted list for the murder of an Egyptian. And to add to boot, following the killing of the Egyptian; in Exodus 2:13, when Moses attempted to reason with a Hebrew as to why he was beating another Hebrew, he was challenged with the questions of who made you a prince and a judge over us? Are you going to kill me like you did the Egyptians? Wow, you talk about being exposed! For something you thought was done in the dark and your dirt has now come to light. You talk about some shenanigans. Now having to face reality and those who know your mess, coupled with trying to lead these very same people who cannot trust you – this is about to be on and popping. So, Moses was already at a disadvantage and was in no shape psychologically to grasp the idea that he was going back to the place where he had fled from. To the very place where the people had no regard for him. Man! This is unthinkable and unfortunate; this is where many of us find ourselves looking for the exit door. Our minds are stuck on stupid, and our brains are scrambled with loose thoughts of having to do, undertake, and/or accomplish what seems insurmountable. Sadly, by default, we make situations bigger than we are when we are bigger than our situations. God is our "X" factor, and He dwells within us through the Holy Spirit Who not only leads us in truth and righteousness but also makes our situations work.

Speaking of work! Elder Michael Price our assistant Pastor has been teaching this one lesson out of 1 Chronicles 28:20, when King David turned over the kingdom to Solomon his son which is also a major undertaking. After giving him instruction King David then tells him to be courageous and do the work. But it gets deeper because Elder Mike and I began to discuss this further and looking at 2 Kings 2:2, where King David tells Solomon his son "...be strong, therefore, and prove yourself as a man." but in a different version of the bible it says, "...act like a man." And in this instance the same is true, Moses is courageous and proves himself as a man. This also holds true for you and me. We need to go out and prove ourselves as to who we are in Christ. Here is the blessing and encouragement for all of us. The minute that God said to Moses I am sending you, automatically put Moses at the advantage and in the winner's circle. This does not mean there would not be any challenges or obstacles to overcome but what it did mean was Romans 8:31, "...if God is for us then who can be against us? Funny that Moses would ask the God of life and all of creation, who am I? Because God already knew who Moses was, but Moses did not know himself or what God hid in him as a treasure (2 Corinthians 4:7).

This very question – who am I? This is one of the many reasons why people quit on a life long before the battle begins because they have no clue as to who they are. Somewhere along life's path many of us have picked up the nasty habits of measuring ourselves against others and their accomplishments shortchanging us of our true essence. When God created us, it was not to measure up against others but instead to mirror His image and likeness. Just remember you were never created to quit but to have dominion and power on the earth; battle the quits.

Chapter 19

THINK IT NOT STRANGE!

Many of you may be unaware of my weekly bible study that occurs Monday thru Friday from 6 am –6:30 am that has been in existence for the past four years; and on one of my recent weekly studies, I was teaching on the love of Christ and referenced 1 Peter 4:8-12. While thinking about the verses, it was at this point that verse 12 stood out to me like a sore thumb as the Apostle Peter said, "Beloved, do not think it strange concerning the fiery trial which is to try you, as though some strange thing happened to you." Here the Apostle Peter is speaking from experience as he pours out this thought in scripture to the believer. Why such a simple yet profound thought? Because Peter went through it himself several times from spiritual mountain highs to mental valley lows throughout his walk with Christ; pre-cross, post-cross, and ascension. Peter had some tests in his life as a Christian and the one that appeared so simple when reading it had the most profound effect on him. I can only think had it not been for Jesus' forewarning Peter in Luke 22:31 of Satan's impending attack Peter would not have known what had hit him. Satan had asked Jesus for Peter to separate him as wheat; and even after being forewarned he was still ill-equipped for what was ahead. The arrogance of Apostle Peter got him in trouble, no different than arrogance will get you and me in trouble when no one can tell us anything. Peter was not hearing Jesus at all when He said Satan wanted to sift him as wheat. My mind would have been all over the place not knowing what the sifting process entailed and how long that season of my life would last from the testing of my faith to the recovery process from such a fiery test. I would have been crying out to Lord why me? In fact, my selfishness would have asked Jesus what about James, John, or one of these other jokers running around here with us lol. But this was purposeful for him. He needed this to break his arrogance and cockiness. Plus, there was great work ahead of him and he needed to be refined and spiritually tuned. This season for him would be one of strengthening and restoration so that in the time to come Peter would do for others what Christ did. The word of God is powerful, transformative, and restorative; and is what we need for change.

As I continue to search out and read the word of God, I want to encourage you to know that everyday life has an offering, a contribution, a gift that is made up of unique factors and characteristics that are not comfortable but meant to empower us, restore us, and transform us if we count them as joy. In other words, if we approach them with an expectation to see God's hand moving in our lives they will prove to work out for our good. No, they are not fun, no they are not pleasant or wrapped in bows. But in many instances, they are what we need to help mature us and minister to us in our trials. These things, these siftings, and everything else improves us as people, so we do not become quitters. I can tell you Peter walked away broken during his test when Satan was attempting to sift him as wheat; and we would experience and go through the same.

So, what are some of life's offerings, contributions, and gifts that you have experienced? Now for clarity's sake I used the word gift in this chapter contrary to what we would normally expect a gift to be. Speaking of gifts, look at what the Apostle says in the next sentence in which I consider a gift. The Apostle Paul records in 2 Corinthians 12:7, that a messenger of Satan was sent to him to buffet him lest he is exalted above measure. Paul said he cried out three times to the Lord to remove the thorn from his flesh, but the Lord said to him that my grace is sufficient for thee in your weakness My power is made perfect. Now his situation is not an everyday occurrence and very few people will ever have the Apostle's challenges. His situation was unique to his experience. He is buffeted to keep him humble and that was a gift contrary to what most would realize. With that said, when life comes at you full steam ahead, horns blowing, and high beams blaring; do not lose focus of the road God has you on; and neither be detoured. God will get you through it as long as you do not give up; in simple, do not quit. Therefore, think it not strange when you go through your test, your storms, God is working it out in you. Battle the quits.

Chapter 20

ALLOW YOURSELF GREATNESS

As this thought of greatness came to mind, I laughed because my immediate supervisor Gloria Wright and I have this running saying, that is in jest and in just; and that is "they won't let you be great". Now the "they" is in general terms and universal to all things in life. For instance, we often talk about our lawns and the work we put into them only to find ourselves fighting a losing battle against the sun and its blazing heat. Thus, in jest quoting "the sun won't allow us to be great" as we laugh. But there are times in life when the climate of this world and its evil will not allow you to be great and that thought is in just. in just because of inequities, hate, and simply plain ole evil people - "people won't allow you to be great"; and that is one of the tragedies of life. And though a man in many instances will do all in his power to impede your greatness in this world especially if you are black; true greatness is not hindered by one's opposition to you or anyone else. Why? Because greatness is the reply, response, and results of those determined to succeed at all costs. It is the antidote to a poisonous and sick world.

I remember teaching a sermon one Sunday, from the book of Romans 12:3, when the Apostle Paul brought to thought something that was very powerful and important pertaining to his life and that of ours as well. In verse 3, the Apostle Paul says, that he was given grace and that he had been dealt a measure of faith by God – wow! I say wow because that grace he received, and that measure of faith dealt to him is what God has given and dealt to each of us. If we could only understand the magnitude of this, our walk with Christ would change from religion to relationship. If we could grasp how these two things are working in us, then we would realize they are the game changers of life; and then we would see ourselves in a different light. Our Christian experience would be marked by the abundance of life that Christ has come to give. We would literally see the hand of God working in and through our situations for our good. Then and only then we could rejoice and count it all joy when we fall into various trials, knowing that the testing of our faith produces patience; and let patience have its perfect work that we are perfect and complete lacking nothing. Knowing that God has put us in perfection (Christ Jesus) while going through imperfection allowing greatness to be achieved. In other words, we who are in Christ are not perfect, but perfection is He who resides on the inside of us; and He is Christ.

Think about it, there are so many great reports and testimonies of people doing great things by this grace and faith given to us by God. So why do we settle for less? Why do we quit and give up? When God has equipped us to be great in Him. Jesus even speaks of us doing great things in Him who believe (John 14:12-14). And if we cannot deny His greatness and power then we should not deny ourselves the experience to be great.

The thought, that God gives us grace has a couple of usages to it. First and foremost, we are afforded mercy, clemency, and pardons for our past behaviors and actions through Jesus Christ our Lord and Savior. This does not mean that we get a free pass in life. Because there are times when we will suffer the repercussion and consequences of our choices. But with that we can get some do-overs and second, third, and fourth chances in life to change and do better; and praise the Lord for that. The second aspect of grace given to us is that we experience God's favor in various aspects of our lives and at different times. By default, we are winners, because we were created in His image and likeness. God gave us dominion over the earth and told us to subdue it. Unfortunately, that is a fleeting thought and not a practiced principle because of bad religion. Do you not know that you were created by God to be great; and that there is no other expectation of you than that of greatness? So, my question becomes to the masses, why don't you give yourself that chance? We certainly know that greatness exists because we see it every day in the lives of so many other people. But we do not see it in ourselves. To many of us falter with fear, low esteem, and feeling inadequate. Not believing in ourselves, not seeing ourselves a better light or condition. We often compare ourselves to others, seeing a dim version of ourselves. God has given us grace in all forms and again each one of us has been dealt a measure of faith. Whatever all that looks like and the AMOUNT to be is more than enough to do some amazing things. And yes, I am preaching to myself first and foremost before I preach it to anyone else. Even with me writing this book, I questioned myself if it would be worth writing comparing myself to others. But as the Lord would have it, if only one person's life is touched by this book then it was worth writing because life is priceless and invaluable.

Allow yourself to be great because greatness lies within you and awaits your permission to be exposed and experienced. What does it require of us to experience this greatness? I cannot begin to stress enough the relationship we must have with Christ Jesus as our Lord and Savior. In this relationship we learn so much about ourselves and Him. The change is incredible and unexplainable. Our outlook, conversations, and awareness of life takes on a new view. With this, we take inventory of our worth and know our value. And through this process we walk in this new creation stepping beyond our past and accessing our future. There are two necessary tools needed for greatness and we have already received them from God; grace and faith. But there are some other key ingredients that are essential that we need to acquire if we have not already done so. These essential ingredients are sacrifice, commitment, perseverance, vision, mental toughness, discipline, and fortitude; and we find all of them in our relationship with Christ. Therefore, I cannot stress enough that all these coupled with grace and faith bring each of us to that place of greatness.

Oh yeah, I forgot one thing, and that is you must divorce yourself from quitting. Quitters never win and winners never quit. So, stop entertaining and defeating yourself with those unproductive thoughts that are self-destructive. Replace those thoughts with words that are positive, powerful, transformative, and enlightening. In essence, speak life to yourself and your situations. And greatness will come knocking. Battle the quits.

Chapter 21

IT IS IN MY HANDS

As I close this book out the power to do is in the palms of our hands. As I considered this thought I was looking across the Atlantic Ocean from my balcony one afternoon in Myrtle Beach. Its vastness and expanse- reaffirmed my belief about our limitless possibilities. It was in this moment I felt in my heart God speaking to me about life in general. It was in this very same moment that a cold chill blanketed my arms begging the question to what and who are you waiting on? Are you expecting a knock on the door, a ringing of the cell phone, or a passerby to say here is what you need to succeed? No doubt these things can happen, but it is not reasonable to think they will. Are you looking across the sky awaiting the finger of God to write in the clouds above your head what the next movement is? It can happen, but who is to say that it will. God has equipped us with everything that we have need of to change course and direction; as well as to experience life in its fullness and abundance. Even Jesus tells us in scripture, Luke 11:9 "For everyone who ask receives, and he who seeks finds, and to him who knocks it will be opened." This scripture pertains to receiving the Holy Spirit. Who is the Holy Spirit? He is the power of God. So even in this when we receive the Holy Spirit, we are empowered to do great things. With that said, I know this next statement has become an exhausted phrase, principle, cliché, adage, and/or thought, but "if you can see it, you can achieve it"; and that is a truism. But unfortunately, our arch enemy (self) blocks our view in this matter with thoughts that signal to us that quitting is our only option when we are flailing or splashing around in ponds of stillness as though this is all we have. Do you not know that God has created oceans for us to sail and rivers to flow through allowing us passage from one point in our lives to the next? He that has made us in Christ Jesus has also made us as captains of our ships (our individual lives). But all too often we choose the paddle boats and ponds because they are still, and easy and safer to navigate. In the narrow mind ponds appear to be one's only option, but we choose them because the water is still and settled. Most people do not like challenges so ponds are it. So, if you like splashing around then play in the ponds that lead to nowhere in life which is equivalent to quitting; so, enjoy the ripples because that will be the extent of your experience. But if you want something greater then it is time to get out of the paddle boat and start walking on water; Peter did so why can't we do the same by faith? It is in your hands, the power to do. I can do all thing through Christ Who strengthens me.

Thank you for hanging out with me in this read. I pray that it has blessed and empowered you to take that next step in your life.

After I completed writing this book, during the editing phase I found out that a childhood friend of mine, Keith Flowers, has been battling cancer for several years now; and that he had just come through a major bout with it. My prayers are for you and your family, my brother. Keep battling, fight the good fight faith, and hold to the promises of God – we win in Christ Jesus. Love you man. (February 20, 2023). Battle the quits.